OCCASIONAL PAPER 116

Improving the International Monetary System

Constraints and Possibilities

Michael Mussa, Morris Goldstein, Peter B. Clark,
Donald J. Mathieson, and Tamim Bayoumi

INTERNATIONAL MONETARY FUND
Washington DC
December 1994

© 1994 International Monetary Fund

Library of Congress Cataloging-in-Publication Data

Improving the international monetary system : constraints and
   possibilities / Michael Mussa . . . [et al.].
      p. cm. — (Occasional Papers, ISSN 0251-6365 ; 116)
   Includes bibliographical references.
   ISBN 1-55775-444-6 : ($15.00, $12.00)
   1. International finance. 2. Foreign exchange rates.   3. Capital
market.   I. Mussa, Michael II. Series: Occasional paper
(International Monetary Fund) ; no. 116.
HG3881.I56   1994

Price: US$15.00
(US$12.00 to full-time faculty members and
students at universities and colleges)

Please send orders to:
International Monetary Fund, Publication Services
700 19th Street, N.W., Washington, D.C. 20431, U.S.A.
Tel.: (202) 623-7430   Telefax: (202) 623-7201

recycled paper

Contents

	Page
Preface	v
I. Introduction	1
II. The Current Exchange Rate Regime	4
Characteristics of the Current Exchange Rate Regime	4
Exchange Rate Developments and Policy Coordination Efforts Since 1973	8
Overall Performance Since 1973	11
III. The Expansion and Integration of International Financial Markets	13
Structural Changes in International Financial Markets	13
Policy Implications of Structural Changes in International Financial Markets	14
IV. Volatility, Misalignment, and Access to Capital	18
Volatility	18
Exchange Rate Misalignments	22
Access to International Capital Markets	24
V. Limiting Exchange Rate Variability: The Target Zone Method	25
Benefits and Costs of Target Zones	25
Policies to Maintain Target Zones	27
The Role of Monetary Policy	29
VI. Conclusions and Implications for the IMF	31
References	35

Tables

Section

II.	1. Developing Countries: Classification of Exchange Rate Arrangements	8
	2. Standard Deviation of Monthly Change in Bilateral Real Exchange Rates	10
	3. Growth in Real Trade and Real GDP	11

Charts

Section

II.	1. Major Industrial Countries: Nominal and Real Effective Exchange Rates, January 1973–June 1994	6
IV.	2. Germany, Japan, and the United States: Volatility of Nominal Exchange Rates, January 1962–July 1994	19
	3. Volatility of Selected Nominal Exchange Rates, January 1962– July 1994	21
	4. United States: Real Exports and Imports of Goods and Services, January 1973–June 1994	23

The following symbols have been used throughout this paper:

... to indicate that data are not available;

— to indicate that the figure is zero or less than half the final digit shown, or that the item does not exist;

– between years or months (e.g., 1991–92 or January–June) to indicate the years or months covered, including the beginning and ending years or months;

/ between years (e.g., 1991/92) to indicate a crop or fiscal (financial) year.

"Billion" means a thousand million.

Minor discrepancies between constituent figures and totals are due to rounding.

The term "country," as used in this paper, does not in all cases refer to a territorial entity that is a state as understood by international law and practice; the term also covers some territorial entities that are not states, but for which statistical data are maintained and provided internationally on a separate and independent basis.

Preface

This study, which was prepared by the Research Department of the IMF, addresses major policy issues associated with the future of the international monetary system. It focuses on whether there is a need for fundamental reform of this system, defined as a systematic and sustained effort on the part of the three major industrial countries to maintain their exchange rates within agreed ranges. It then discusses less far-reaching reforms that could strengthen and improve the system.

This study was prompted, in part, by the fiftieth anniversary of the international conference held at Bretton Woods, New Hampshire, in July 1944, and by the debate about the future of the international monetary system that this anniversary engendered. Much of the existing international institutional framework was created at Bretton Woods, namely, the International Monetary Fund and the International Bank for Reconstruction and Development (the World Bank). Fifty years is probably an appropriate moment to take stock of international monetary arrangements, and this paper summarizes the views of the authors as a contribution to the debate about this important topic.

All of the authors are members of the Research Department of the IMF. Michael Mussa is the Director of the Department, Morris Goldstein is Deputy Director, Peter Clark and Donald Mathieson are Division Chiefs, and Tamim Bayoumi is an economist. The authors wish to thank Youkyong Kwon and Susanna Mursula for research assistance, Gail Blade and Lena Buckle for secretarial aid, and numerous colleagues, in particular Steven Symansky, for comments and advice. Thanks are also due to Thomas Walter of the External Relations Department, who edited the manuscript and coordinated publication, and Alicia Etchebarne-Bourdin of the External Relations Department, who provided typesetting assistance.

An earlier version of this paper was discussed by the Executive Board of the IMF, and the text was revised in the light of the many useful comments in that discussion. The opinions expressed in this paper, however, are those of the authors and do not necessarily reflect the views of the IMF or its Executive Directors.

I Introduction

With the celebration of the fiftieth anniversary of the Bretton Woods Conference in July 1994, attention has naturally focused on the performance of, and suggestions for improvements in, the international monetary system. The Articles of Agreement of the IMF, which spell out the rules that govern the international monetary system, make clear that it is a means of promoting international trade in goods and services, as well as capital flows, with the objective of achieving high levels of sustainable economic growth and stability across the international economy. Hence, the functioning of the international monetary system cannot be assessed as an end in itself. Rather, it needs to be assessed in terms of how well it promotes the ultimate objectives of economic growth and stability. Consequently, proposals for reform of the system should be evaluated in terms of the extent to which they will contribute to achieving these underlying objectives. As the central international monetary institution, the IMF has the key role of overseeing the system and ensuring that members fulfill their obligations toward the IMF and each other so as to facilitate the achievement of these objectives.

Two key interrelated parts of the international monetary system are exchange rates and capital flows. The Bretton Woods system, which was in place from 1946 to 1973, put much more emphasis on the former part; the system was primarily concerned with promoting stability in exchange rates and in economic conditions more broadly, so that the chaotic situation of the 1930s regarding trade and international payments would not be repeated in the postwar world. What was not then foreseen was the extraordinary expansion in international capital markets over time. As private capital flows have come to play a key role in determining exchange rates and financing external imbalances in many countries, a discussion of possible improvements in the international monetary system must consider both exchange rate arrangements and the role of capital flows for the functioning of the system.

In contrast to the Bretton Woods fixed exchange rate system, an important feature of the current international monetary system is the diversity of exchange rate arrangements. In particular, bilateral exchange rates between the three largest industrial nations—the United States, Japan, and Germany—have operated under a regime of managed floating since the early 1970s. Under this regime, the authorities are not indifferent to the behavior of their currencies. Official intervention, both unilateral and coordinated, is used by all three countries at times to influence their exchange rates. On occasion, macroeconomic policies, including monetary policy, are adjusted in light of exchange rate developments, and these three countries, in concert with the other major industrial countries, have at times coordinated these actions. However, no consistent, determined effort is made to adjust their economic policies with the intent of keeping their exchange rates within announced and relatively narrow limits or ranges. These three large countries have generally accepted fluctuations in their bilateral exchange rates across quite wide ranges and have oriented their basic economic policies primarily toward other objectives.

Other countries are able to choose the exchange rate arrangements that are deemed most appropriate for their particular circumstances. Participants in the exchange rate mechanism (ERM) of the European Monetary System (EMS), for example, have agreed to limit the variation in their bilateral exchange rates within set bands, while many other countries, particularly in the developing world, choose to peg their rates against specific currencies or baskets of currencies.

This decentralized and flexible system has proved quite resilient in the face of economic disturbances and trends. It was able to cope with the oil crises in 1973 and 1979 without experiencing significant strains in exchange markets, despite the relatively divergent macroeconomic responses across countries to these events. The system has likewise accommodated the different cyclical conditions experienced by many countries in the 1980s and early 1990s. More generally, it has adapted relatively smoothly to secular trends in the world economy, including the expansion in the breadth and depth of private capital markets

I INTRODUCTION

over time and the growing importance of Japan and Europe in world capital markets.

That being said, some observers have regarded the performance of the existing international monetary system as disappointing and possibly inferior to what might be achieved by greater fixity of exchange rates and more homogeneity in exchange arrangements. Their concerns have been focused in several areas. First, under floating exchange arrangements, exchange rates have been highly volatile.[1] It is not unusual for key currency exchange rates to move by several percent over the period of a few weeks—a level of variability that is thought by many to be disruptive of international trade and investment. Second, it is often asserted that nominal and real exchange rates have too frequently been subject to significant misalignments, that is, to situations whereby exchange rates either become divorced from economic fundamentals or reflect inappropriate and unsustainable economic policies. The clearest example of such a misalignment was the appreciation of the U.S. dollar in 1984–85. Some economists would cite the appreciation of the pound sterling in 1979–81 and the behavior of the yen since early 1993 as other examples of misalignments of floating exchange rate currencies. Although not directly related to exchange rate arrangements, abrupt changes in the access of developing countries to private capital markets have also been a cause for concern—most notably the reduced access experienced during the debt crisis of the early 1980s, but also the movement in the opposite direction in the early 1990s—leading to questions about the ability of such markets to provide capital appropriately to developing countries. A common theme in these concerns is some skepticism about the ability of private capital markets to respond to events in a manner that reflects economic fundamentals.

As the main features of the international monetary system, as well as proposals for reform, have been dealt with at length elsewhere, this paper provides a selective discussion of the issues involved.[2] Section II gives a brief overview of the key characteristics of the current exchange rate regime. This is followed in Section III by a summary of the evolution of international capital markets since the collapse of the Bretton Woods system.[3] Possible defects in the current international monetary system—excessive exchange rate volatility, proclivity to misalignment, and abrupt changes in access to international capital markets—are then examined in Section IV. Some approaches to dealing with these possible deficiencies are discussed in Section V, and the final section—Section VI—presents the paper's conclusions, including implications for the role of the IMF.

A central issue discussed in this paper is the extent to which fundamental reform of the international monetary system is feasible or desirable at present. In this paper, "fundamental reform" refers to a systematic and sustained effort on the part of the three major industrial countries to maintain their exchange rates within agreed ranges. The staff of the IMF has for some time set forth views on this topic based on extensive analysis of the operation of the international monetary system.[4] This paper summarizes those views in an effort to prompt a debate, with the recognition that other serious schools of thought are more sympathetic to the need for, and prospect of, fundamental reform. It is hoped that this debate will help to delineate areas of agreement and of disagreement and to contribute to an understanding of the measures that might be taken to improve the performance of the international monetary system, whether or not these measures might be characterized as "fundamental reform."

With regard to the feasibility of fundamental reform, the key question is whether the three largest countries are prepared to assign to monetary policy the primary task of keeping their exchange rates within relatively narrow ranges. (The use of other policies for this task is discussed below.) In their policy choices to date, the authorities in these countries appear to have demonstrated a clear preference for using monetary policy primarily for the purpose of domestic stabilization, that is, for pursuing the ultimate objectives of sustainable growth with low inflation. Moreover, it seems unlikely that a new European Central Bank, charged with the mandate of pursuing price stability in the European Union (EU), would want to compromise achieving this objective by taking on ambitious exchange rate objectives vis-à-vis the other two major (non-Union, non-European) currencies.

Although, owing to its flexibility and effectiveness, monetary policy is the most potent instrument for achieving exchange rate objectives, the question arises as to whether other available policy instruments could substitute reliably for monetary policy in pursuing this external assignment. Fiscal policy is not generally suitable for this task; it is too inflexible, it should not be deflected from its appropriate medium-term objectives, and it has too uncertain a relationship to exchange rates to be relied

---

[1] See Mussa (1990) for a discussion of this increase in volatility.
[2] See Frenkel and Goldstein (1986, 1991); Frenkel, Goldstein, and Masson (1991); Aghevli, Khan, and Montiel (1991); and Crockett and Goldstein (1987).
[3] For an extensive discussion of the integration of national capital markets, see Goldstein and Mussa (1993).

[4] See International Monetary Fund (1984b, 1984c); Crockett and Goldstein (1987); Aghevli, Khan, and Montiel (1991); Frenkel, Goldstein, and Masson (1991); and Goldstein and others (1992).

upon.[5] Sterilized exchange market intervention may be useful for helping to calm disorderly markets, and even, on occasion, for sending signals to the markets about policy intentions and exchange rate objectives. However, it is simply not potent enough in today's world of enormous and agile private international capital flows to manage exchange rates on its own when the markets have a concerted and determined view that a prevailing exchange rate is not sustainable. Finally, controls on international capital flows run counter to the efficient allocation of global saving and are unlikely to be effective in influencing exchange rates unless implemented on a near universal basis—a most unlikely outcome. Recall, for example, that two of the world's six largest exchange markets (Hong Kong and Singapore) are located outside the Group of Ten countries.

With regard to the desirability of seeking fundamental reform of the international monetary system at present, a number of considerations are relevant. First, if exchange rate management were given top priority by the three largest industrial countries in the orientation of monetary policy, there could well be costs in terms of their ability to achieve sustainable growth with low inflation. Given the cyclical differences among these countries and the country-specific shocks affecting them in recent years, significant external constraints on the conduct of monetary policy could well have been counterproductive in terms of the ultimate goals of that policy. Nor is it clear that the benefits to the rest of the world from increased exchange rate stability in the major currencies would outweigh the costs created by the reduced possibilities to stabilize output and inflation in these countries. Second, the present system already allows those countries for which exchange rate stability takes on particularly high importance to participate in regional arrangements that limit the degree of exchange rate variability. Third, there is ample scope within the present exchange rate system for fostering conditions more favorable to greater exchange rate stability. Specifically, improvements in the design and implementation of domestic economic policies—particularly in the fiscal and structural areas—are the most viable and effective means for alleviating the symptoms of poor systemic performance.

It is particularly in this third area that the IMF has an important role to play in improving the functioning of the present system. In many respects, this system, with its diverse exchange arrangements and immense stocks of mobile capital, makes surveillance by the IMF even more challenging than during the Bretton Woods system of pegged rates and limited capital flows. While the increased size and mobility of private capital has meant that private market surveillance of errant economic policies is now a more potent instrument than before, experience suggests that market discipline does not always occur at an early enough stage. Therefore, strengthened IMF surveillance can make an important contribution by encouraging the timely implementation of underlying policy adjustments—before private market participants force these adjustments to be made on a more costly basis. In this connection, it is relevant to note that neither pegged exchange arrangements nor floating rates have proved completely successful over the past decade or so in disciplining errant fiscal or structural policies. In a similar vein, there is room for increasing the IMF's role as the main forum for international monetary cooperation, so that episodes of exchange rate behavior unrelated to economic fundamentals—or other specific exchange rate policy issues—can be discussed and evaluated, thereby helping to bring about cooperative solutions.

The route to effective reform of the international monetary system does not lie in attempts to directly impose greater exchange rate stability. Rather, the key to achieving this objective—which should not be seen as an end in itself, in part because equilibrium real exchange rates can and do change over time—is provided by improvements in national policies fostered by international cooperation. IMF surveillance should focus on getting the domestic fundamentals right, including monetary policy aiming at price stability, fiscal discipline, and structural policies that promote the efficient working of labor and other markets. Better policies will, in turn, be conducive to the convergence of economic performance in the form of low inflation, higher saving, and improved growth performance on a sustained basis. The cooperative and coordinated pursuit of these objectives through IMF surveillance will thereby tend both to encourage greater exchange stability for those currencies that are floating and minimize exchange market crises and pressures for currencies that are pegged.

---

[5]As discussed below, this is not inconsistent with the need to implement sound medium-term fiscal policies that will foster conditions conducive to greater exchange rate stability.

II The Current Exchange Rate Regime

The current exchange rate system came about as a result of the collapse of the Bretton Woods system of fixed but adjustable exchange rates.[6] Under the Bretton Woods system, countries generally pegged their exchange rates within narrow margins (plus or minus 1 percent) against the U.S. dollar, while the value of the U.S. dollar was fixed in terms of gold. Exchange rates were maintained near their pegs by using official reserve assets in exchange market intervention and by influencing private capital flows through both changes in domestic policies and outright controls on capital movements. Changes in the pegs were subject to international surveillance by the IMF and permitted only under conditions of "fundamental disequilibrium." This system, which was initiated at the Bretton Woods conference in 1944, served the world quite well through the early 1960s, as it provided agreed rules of conduct that were widely shared and thereby imparted a stability to the postwar trading system that was notably absent in the 1930s. However, the underlying tensions in the system became evident during the late 1960s. This tension reflected a number of factors, including the expansionary nature of U.S. macroeconomic policy, the increase in the resources available to private capital markets in relation to official reserve holdings, and divergences in policy objectives among some of the major participants in the system.[7] Despite attempts to maintain the system in the early 1970s, agreed parities between the currencies of the major industrial countries were finally abandoned in early 1973.

Characteristics of the Current Exchange Rate Regime

The Bretton Woods system was replaced by an exchange rate system of managed floating, especially between the three major currencies, which has continued to the present. One characteristic of the current system is that countries are free to choose their own bilateral exchange rate relationships. This was codified in the Second Amendment to the Articles of Agreement of the IMF, as stated in Section 2(b) of Article IV:

> Under an international monetary system of the kind prevailing on January 1, 1976, exchange arrangements may include (i) the maintenance by a member of a value for its currency in terms of the special drawing right or another denominator, other than gold, selected by the member, or (ii) cooperative arrangements by which members maintain the value of their currencies in relation to the value of the currency or currencies of other members, or (iii) other exchange arrangements of a member's choice.

The choice of exchange rate regime reflects to a considerable extent individual countries' assessments of the benefits and costs of a fixed or flexible exchange rate.[8] The benefits that can stem from a fixed but adjustable exchange rate regime typically include enhanced trading and investing opportunities with the other countries within the arrangement, owing to reduced uncertainty, and the stability that a nominal anchor in the form of a pegged rate can provide for monetary policy and inflation expectations. The main cost of such an arrangement is the loss of flexibility in orienting policies toward achieving domestic rather than exchange rate objectives. While these costs may be relatively small if the country in question experiences underlying disturbances similar to those in countries against which it is fixing its exchange rate, they are likely to increase substantially in the face of shocks that impinge only on its economy, although such disturbances can be dealt with by changes in the parity. These considerations, which predict that fixed exchange rates are more likely to develop in regions of the world with close economic ties and similar disturbances, form the basis

---

[6]The papers in Bordo and Eichengreen (1993) provide a detailed discussion of many aspects of the Bretton Woods system.

[7]Garber (1993) and Solomon (1982) discuss the factors that led to the breakup of the Bretton Woods system.

[8]There are some limits on the options available. In particular, as each of the three largest countries allows its exchange rate to float against the others', smaller countries do not have the option of participating in a global system of pegged rates.

Characteristics of the Current Exchange Rate Regime

of the literature on optimum currency areas.[9] As countries face different economic circumstances, the result is a mixed international monetary system in which some countries allow their exchange rates to float relatively freely while others fix the value of their currency against another currency or basket of currencies.

The defining characteristic of the present system, however, is the existence of floating exchange rates between the world's three most important currencies. While the external values of their currencies are not a matter of indifference to these countries, as shown by the Plaza Agreement of 1985 and the Louvre Accord of 1987, significant fluctuations in the relative values of the dollar, yen, and deutsche mark have occurred throughout the floating exchange rate period. Clearly, the three largest industrial countries have not felt a strong need to stabilize their bilateral exchange rates.[10] In particular, they make no consistent or determined effort to manipulate domestic economic policies with the intent of constraining exchange rates within relatively narrow limits.

Several smaller industrial countries also have floating exchange rates, most notably Australia, Canada, New Zealand, and Switzerland. In the aftermath of the European exchange rate crises of 1992–93, Finland, Italy, Norway, Sweden, and the United Kingdom have also adopted this arrangement. This decision does not imply that the level of the exchange rate is unimportant for these countries. In Canada, for example, the level of the exchange rate is clearly perceived as a key macroeconomic variable. Official intervention is used to moderate exchange rate movements ("leaning against the wind"), and the authorities take into account exchange rate movements in formulating and implementing monetary policy. However, while the behavior of the exchange rate may at times affect decisions regarding domestic policies, economic policy is not explicitly geared toward maintaining a particular value or range of values for the currency. The same approach generally applies to other countries with floating exchange rates.

The most important regional arrangement for limiting exchange rate fluctuations is the ERM. When instituted in 1979, the ERM was seen largely as a method of reducing the volatility in exchange rates between European currencies following the breakdown of the Bretton Woods fixed exchange rate system. In the early 1980s, however, the focus switched to controlling inflation, with realignments becoming less frequent and smaller than the persistence of underlying inflation differentials would have warranted.[11] Most recently, the ERM has been seen as an essential part of the movement toward economic integration of the EU. Membership in the ERM is one of the explicit conditions for entry into the European Monetary Union written into the Treaty on European Union, which was signed in February 1992.

Until the period of sustained market pressures starting in September 1992, the ERM had worked well in successfully reducing exchange rate volatility between members, providing a useful nominal anchor for high-inflation countries, and encouraging economic integration. In particular, between early 1987 and early 1992, the ERM became both more anchored and more broadly based, in that there were no changes in parities and a number of new currencies either joined the ERM itself (the pound sterling, peseta, and escudo all joined in 1990) or, in the case of the currencies of the Nordic countries, were unilaterally pegged against the European Currency Unit (ECU). However, the ERM came under sustained market pressures starting in mid-1992, as cyclical divergences, caused in part by the macroeconomic consequences of German reunification, led to conflicts between the domestic and external requirements for monetary policy in both Germany and the other member countries of the ERM. These pressures led Italy and the United Kingdom to suspend their ERM membership; Finland, Norway, and Sweden to abandon their pegs to the ECU; and Spain and Portugal to devalue their parities. Continuing speculative pressures in the summer of 1993 led to a widening of the intervention bands to their current values of 15 percent (except for the rate of the Netherlands guilder against the deutsche mark).

Exchange arrangements in developing countries are also varied. In addition to the considerations already discussed in relation to industrial countries, developing countries must also take into account large terms of trade shocks and thin underlying financial markets in choosing the appropriate exchange rate regime. As can be seen from Table 1, about 55 percent of developing countries, including many smaller countries, pegged the value of their currencies to the currencies of other countries or baskets of other currencies in 1992—an arrangement that provides a nominal anchor for the conduct of monetary policy. Meanwhile, the remaining

---

[9]This literature was initiated by Mundell (1961). Taken literally, the literature refers to the option of permanently fixing exchange rates through a common currency. However, most of the arguments are also relevant for the choice between fixed but adjustable and floating exchange rates. See Goldstein and others (1992) and Tavlas (1993) for surveys of the literature.

[10]See Goldstein and others (1992) for further discussion of this point.

[11]Ungerer and others (1986, 1990) discuss the ERM in considerable detail.

II THE CURRENT EXCHANGE RATE REGIME

Chart 1. Major Industrial Countries: Nominal and Real Effective Exchange Rates, January 1973–June 1994
(1985 = 100; logarithmic scale)

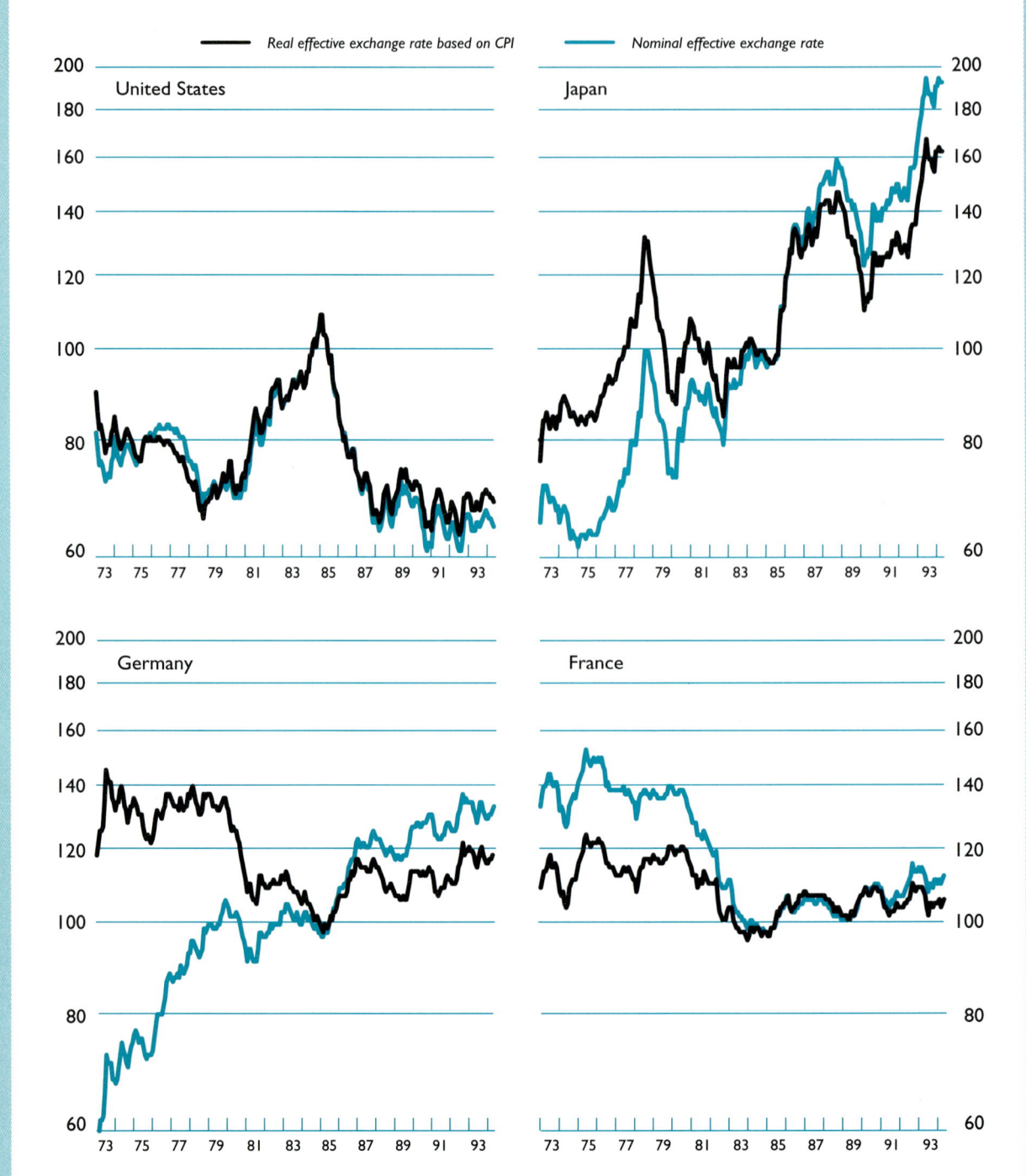

Characteristics of the Current Exchange Rate Regime

Chart 1 *(concluded)*

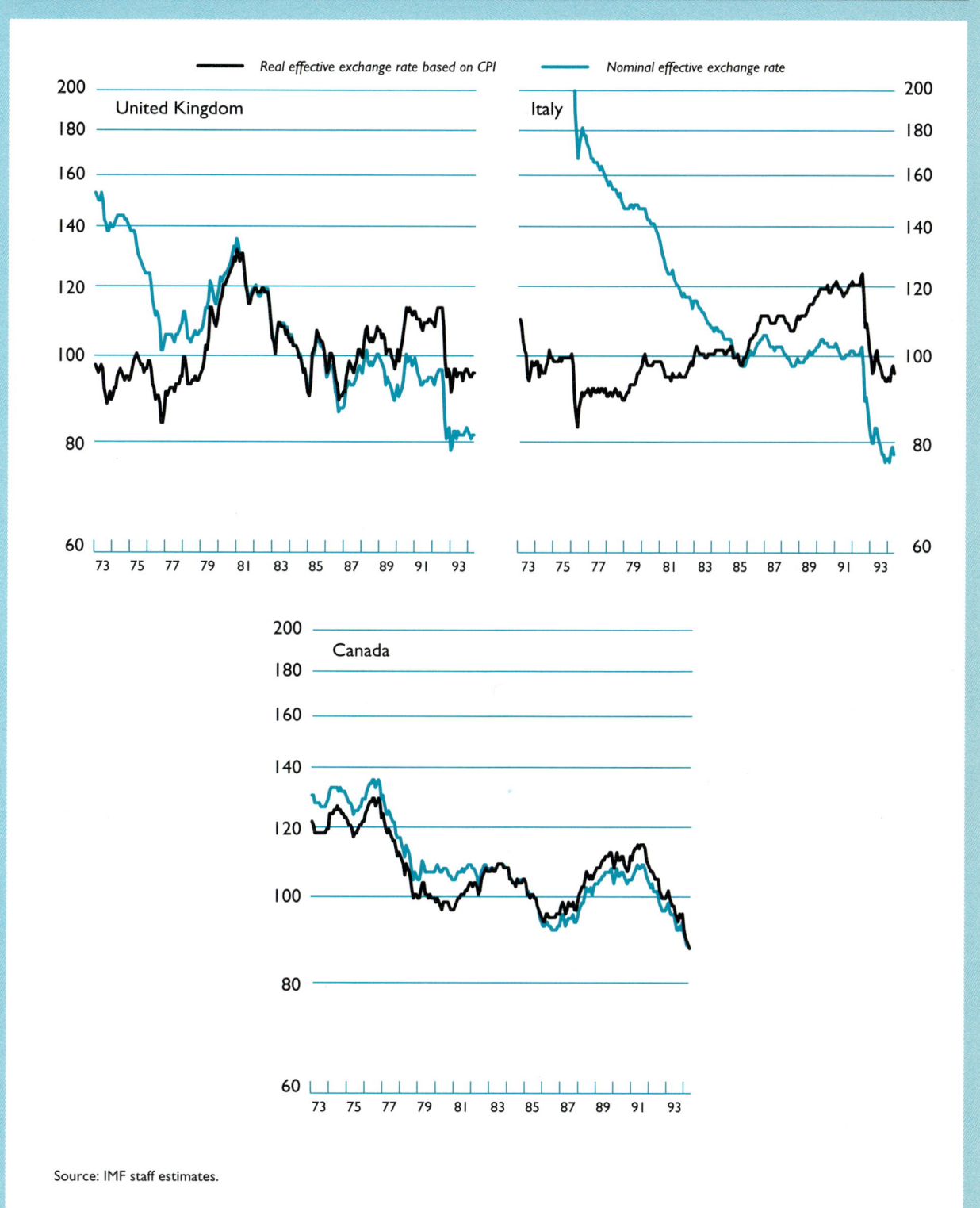

Source: IMF staff estimates.

II THE CURRENT EXCHANGE RATE REGIME

Table 1. Developing Countries: Classification of Exchange Rate Arrangements
(In percent of total number of countries)

	1976	1979	1983	1989	1992
Pegged to a single currency	62.6	52.1	43.5	38.2	36.6
U.S. dollar	43.0	35.0	29.0	23.7	16.7
French franc	12.1	12.0	10.5	10.7	9.0
Pound sterling	2.8	2.6	0.8	—	—
Other currencies	4.7	2.5	3.2	3.8	10.9
Pegged to composite	23.4	23.1	28.2	28.2	18.6
SDR	10.3	11.1	11.3	5.3	1.9
Other (currency basket)	13.1	12.0	16.9	22.9	16.7
Flexible arrangements	14.0	24.8	28.3	33.6	44.8
Adjusting to indicators	5.6	3.4	4.0	3.8	1.9
Others[1]	8.4	21.4	24.3	29.8	42.9
Total	100.0	100.0	100.0	100.0	100.0

Sources: Aghevli, Khan, and Montiel (1991); and International Monetary Fund (1993).
[1] Includes the following categories: "flexibility limited vis-à-vis single currency," "managed floating," and "independently floating."

45 percent of developing countries used more flexible exchange rate arrangements.[12]

These arrangements have a significant regional pattern, with countries in Africa and the Middle East generally adopting pegged exchange rates and Asian countries more prone to employ flexible arrangements. In Europe and the Western Hemisphere both types of arrangements are evident. Low-inflation countries are generally associated with pegged rates and high-inflation countries with more flexible arrangements. The percentage of countries adopting flexible exchange rates has risen steadily over time, reflecting both the higher rates of domestic inflation in developing countries during the 1980s and the uncertainty engendered by fluctuations in the values of the major currencies.[13] The latter factor indicates that the policy regimes in the major industrial countries can affect the behavior of smaller countries.

Exchange Rate Developments and Policy Coordination Efforts Since 1973

Exchange Rate Developments

Chart 1 shows real and nominal multilateral exchange rates since 1973 for the seven largest industrial economies. The oil price shock in 1973 produced some divergent movements in these exchange rates. The major policy concern, however, was recycling the large increase in the revenues of the oil exporting countries, not exchange rate values.[14] By 1977, however, large emerging current account imbalances led an effort to "talk down" the U.S. dollar. The depreciation of the dollar that occurred vis-à-vis the yen and the deutsche mark was eventually regarded as having gone beyond the levels implied by the economic fundamentals; for example, the yen appreciated by 30 percent in real effective terms between August 1977 and August 1978 despite repeated official intervention. By November 1, 1978, a "dollar rescue" package was announced, including a $30 billion fund to be used for intervention to support the dollar. About this time, the dollar started to appreciate—a move that was accelerated by the Iranian revolution in December 1978 and the second oil price hike in June 1979—and, by August 1979, the yen was back to about its level of two years earlier in real effective terms (Chart 1).

The second oil price hike is also generally regarded as contributing to the 35 percent real effective appreciation of the pound sterling between mid-1979 and early 1981. As the United Kingdom was self-sufficient in oil, an increase in the oil price was clearly beneficial

---
[12] Within this group, over one half are classified as floating independently, while most of the rest use a managed floating arrangement.
[13] See Aghevli, Khan, and Montiel (1991) for a discussion of the factors affecting the choice of exchange rate arrangements on the part of developing countries.

[14] As already noted, there was concern about the volatility of exchange rates within Europe, resulting in the formation of the European "snake" arrangement in 1972 and, later, the exchange rate mechanism of the EMS in 1979.

for the pound sterling relative to other major currencies. At the same time, the restrictive monetary policy of the new Government also put upward pressure on the currency. The result was a rapid appreciation of the currency between mid-1979 and early 1981, followed by a relatively gradual decline over the next few years.

The period between 1981 and 1985 was dominated by the steady appreciation of the U.S. dollar, reflecting the expansionary fiscal policy of the Reagan Administration, the successful efforts of monetary policy to bring about a durable reduction in inflation, and a "hands-off" policy with respect to the exchange value of the dollar. Much of this rise in the dollar was regarded with equanimity by the U.S. Administration, in part because it helped to lower inflation during 1981–82 and keep it low during the recovery from the 1982 recession. However, the continuing appreciation of the dollar through 1984 and early 1985 led to increasing concern both inside and outside the United States, as the effects of the appreciated dollar became apparent in large current account imbalances of the major industrial countries, rising protectionist sentiments in the United States, and inflationary pressures in other countries.

This concern prompted coordinated international action by the largest industrial economies to reduce the exchange value of the U.S. dollar.[15] While the dollar had already depreciated steadily from its peak in February 1985, the finance ministers and central bank governors of the United States, Japan, Germany, France, and the United Kingdom met on September 22, 1985, at the Plaza Hotel in New York and issued a communiqué that stated that "some further orderly appreciation in the nondollar currencies is desirable" and that they would "stand ready to cooperate more closely to encourage this when to do so would be helpful." The communiqué did not specify in any detail how this exchange rate movement was to be accomplished, except to say that Japanese monetary policy should "exercise flexible management with due attention to the yen exchange rate." On the Monday that the Plaza Agreement, as it became known, was made public, the dollar fell by 4 percent against a weighted average of all currencies and by slightly larger levels against the yen and the deutsche mark. The next morning, substantial intervention to encourage this downward movement was reported to have occurred. The dollar then continued to depreciate at about the same rate that had occurred between February and September 1985; this decline was facilitated by a fall in U.S. interest rates and continued multilateral exchange market intervention.[16]

By September 1986, the U.S. dollar had fallen from its peak of 260 yen to the dollar to 154 yen, and the German and Japanese authorities had started to intervene with the object of supporting the dollar. Subsequently, the dollar continued to decline despite an agreement between the U.S. and Japanese authorities, made public on October 31, 1986, to stabilize the exchange rate of the dollar against the yen in its current range, and for Japan to undertake a fiscal expansion. As concern mounted that the dollar's decline could become excessive, the finance ministers and central bank governors of the Group of Six industrial countries met at the Louvre in Paris on February 21–22, 1987. The communiqué of what became known as the Louvre Accord indicated that the dollar and other currencies should be stabilized "around current levels" because "the ministers and governors agreed that the substantial exchange rate changes since the Plaza Agreement will increasingly contribute to reducing external imbalances and have brought their currencies within ranges broadly consistent with underlying economic fundamentals. . . . Further substantial exchange rate shifts among their currencies could damage growth and adjustment prospects in their countries." These objectives were supported by intervention on the part of a number of central banks, both before and after the meeting, and by the implementation of agreed macroeconomic policies involving an expansion of Japanese domestic demand and tax cuts by several European countries, including Germany.

In public, the participants of the Louvre meeting denied that any target range for the exchange rates had been set. However, Funabashi (1988, pp. 183–87) reported that they discussed a "reference range" of 5 percent around the then current levels of their exchange rates, as well as the obligations that movements outside this range would entail. If such limits were established, they were soon violated by the continued decline in the U.S. dollar. This depreciation persisted through 1987 partly on account of some apparently conflicting statements by authorities in the major industrial countries before the October 19, 1987 stock market crash and the easing of U.S. monetary policy after the crash.

Opinions on the effectiveness of the Plaza Agreement and Louvre Accord differ significantly. Some believe that the Plaza Agreement, together with earlier and later meetings of the largest industrial economies, was an important factor in the decline in the

---

[15]See Funabashi (1988) for an extensive discussion of these actions.

[16]Further macroeconomic coordination occurred in March and April 1986, when simultaneous reductions in discount rates were announced by the major central banks, with the aim of stimulating the world economy.

II THE CURRENT EXCHANGE RATE REGIME

Table 2. Standard Deviation of Monthly Change in Bilateral Real Exchange Rates[1]
(In percent)

	1962–72	1973–78	1979–86	1987–94
Yen/U.S. dollar	1.0	3.1	3.5	3.2
Deutsche mark/U.S. dollar	0.8	3.7	3.5	3.5
Deutsche mark/yen	1.0	3.1	3.2	3.0
Canadian dollar/U.S. dollar	0.6	1.3	1.4	1.4
Swiss franc/deutsche mark	0.9	2.5	1.6	1.3
Dutch guilder/deutsche mark	1.1	1.4	0.7	0.7
French franc/deutsche mark	1.4	2.1	1.3	0.6
Pound sterling/deutsche mark	1.7	3.1	3.2	2.3

Source: IMF staff estimates.
[1] Real exchange rates are calculated using consumer price indices. Data for 1994 extend through June for all exchange rates except for the Netherlands guilder, which extend through May.

U.S. dollar from its peak.[17] These commentators also see the Louvre Accord as taking an important step to slow the decline of the dollar during 1987. Others are more skeptical, arguing that the Plaza Agreement had little to do with the decline in the dollar, which, in their view, was a market correction that would have occurred independently of the behavior of governments. Furthermore, this latter group considers that the attempt to halt the decline of the dollar in 1987 may have helped to precipitate the stock market crash in October of that year by creating an expectation that the Federal Reserve would raise interest rates.[18]

In the weeks following the stock market crash, the U.S. dollar declined to new lows against the deutsche mark and the yen, as U.S. economic policy focused primarily on domestic economic and financial stability. However, beginning in 1988, the Group of Seven industrial countries resumed efforts at international policy coordination. In general, as reflected in periodic communiqués, the Group of Seven discussions covered the broad range of macroeconomic policy issues of interest to the participating countries, and exchange rates issues were considered in this broader macroeconomic context. From time to time, specific efforts were directed at resisting exchange rate movements regarded as unwarranted by fundamentals and contrary to policy objectives. These efforts were sometimes announced in communiqués, but they did not involve formal commitments to target ranges for exchange rates and were generally perceived as less ambitious than the Louvre Accord. Official intervention—including coordinated intervention by two or more of the central banks of the largest industrial countries—was used to resist movements in the major currencies on a number of occasions from early 1988 through as recently as June 1994.

Policy Coordination Efforts

The impact and effectiveness of efforts at international policy coordination by the leading industrial countries since the Louvre Accord are somewhat difficult to evaluate, especially in light of the broad range of macroeconomic issues that these efforts cover. On the one hand, focusing narrowly on the issue of exchange rate volatility, the short-term variability of exchange rates between the three major currencies in the period since the Louvre Accord is essentially the same as it was in earlier subperiods, going back to the beginning of generalized floating in 1973 (Table 2). On the other hand, and probably more important, it would appear from the paths of the real effective exchange rates of the U.S. dollar and the deutsche mark (Chart 1) that episodes of serious overvaluation or undervaluation, particularly of the dollar—as took place in the years before 1987—have been successfully avoided in recent years. By contrast, this result is less clear with regard to misalignments of the yen, in view of its strong real effective appreciation since the summer of 1992. However, as shown in Chart 1, there appears to be a noticeable upward trend in the real effective exchange rate of

---
[17] For example, Funabashi (1988) and Dominguez and Frankel (1993).
[18] Feldstein (1988) and Krugman (1988).

Table 3. Growth in Real Trade and Real GDP
(Average annual growth rates in percent)

	1963–73		1973–93	
	Real Trade[1]	Real GDP	Real Trade[1]	Real GDP
Industrial countries	9.5	4.7	3.9	2.3
United States	8.6	4.0	4.6	2.3
Japan	14.7	9.3	4.6	3.6
Germany	10.2	4.5	3.5	1.9
Developing countries	7.1	6.3	4.6	3.9
Africa	6.3	4.9	0.9	2.3
Asia	9.0	6.4	9.4	6.1
Middle East and Europe	11.2	8.9	–0.1	3.1
Western Hemisphere	3.3	6.3	4.5	2.9

Source: IMF staff estimates.
[1] Real trade is defined as the sum of real merchandise exports and real merchandise imports.

the yen; the most recent appreciation may therefore reflect in part a continuation of this trend.

Moreover, it is not clear that the record of misalignments since 1987 represents a significant change from the 1973–80 floating rate period. It may simply be that the economic forces that contributed importantly to the large misalignments of the U.S. dollar between 1980 and 1987—notably the upsurge and subsequent reduction of U.S. inflation and the mix of monetary and fiscal policies implemented in the early 1980s—have not recurred in recent years. Alternatively, it could well be that policy coordination itself helps to forestall the policy errors and imbalances that contribute to serious exchange rate misalignments. In addition, the signals sent by official communiqués and by exchange market intervention may have helped to counteract "bandwagon" effects and other market anomalies that would otherwise have led in recent years to wider swings in exchange rates.

In any event, given the costly experience with serious exchange rate misalignments in the past, there seems to be greater determination among the authorities of major industrial countries to avoid such misalignments—and the policies that contribute to them—in the future. There is now a strong consensus that monetary policies need to focus on the objective of achieving reasonable price stability over the medium term and, accordingly, avoid contributing to the cycles of inflation and disinflation that have been a major source of macroeconomic instability. With the convergence of inflation rates to very low levels in all the major industrial countries, one of the key factors that presumably contributed to past exchange rate instability would be removed. In addition, serious and persistent efforts to reduce fiscal deficits and to put the ratios of public debt to GDP on a downward track should contribute to confidence and overall stability in financial markets, including foreign exchange markets. Thus, as a consequence of both macroeconomic policies better directed toward attaining the key objectives of sustainable growth with reasonable price stability and improved efforts at policy coordination among the largest industrial countries, it is to be hoped that the international monetary system is evolving toward greater exchange rate stability between the major currencies.

Overall Performance Since 1973

Seen from a broad perspective, the underlying economic performance in the period since 1973 has been mixed.[19] There has been a continuing expansion of trade in goods and services, both in absolute terms and as a ratio to output (Table 3). The period has also seen a significant expansion in capital flows between economies, as net saving in some countries has been made increasingly available for investment in others.[20] At the same time, economic performance, as measured by the two most basic macroeconomic indicators—inflation and growth in real output—has been somewhat disappointing. Inflation rose sharply after 1973 in many countries,

---
[19] Bordo (1993) and Bayoumi and Eichengreen (1994) provide a comparison of economic performance under the current system with that during earlier exchange rate regimes.
[20] This development is discussed in the following section.

II THE CURRENT EXCHANGE RATE REGIME

in part because of macroeconomic responses to the oil price hikes. More recently, the industrial countries appear to have returned to a period of sustained low inflation, but the same cannot be said for developing countries.

As far as the growth in real output is concerned, it is still unclear how far the decline in performance since 1973 reflects an autonomous return to long-term trends after the "catch-up" from the devastation of two world wars, as opposed to other, more immediate factors.[21] However, there is little hard evidence that the slowdown in growth was caused by problems in the international monetary system. The slowdown in economic growth that occurred broadly in the industrial countries after the early 1970s is generally attributed in the economic literature to a significant slowdown in the rate of total factor productivity growth. It is very difficult to establish any link between the slowdown in productivity growth and the change in the nature of the international monetary system, and most economists who have sought to explain economic growth do not point to this particular factor.[22] Moreover, a number of economies, particularly in Asia, have experienced exceptionally rapid growth since the early 1970s despite the change in the nature of the international monetary system. More generally, trade has continued to expand faster than output in most regions of the world (Table 3), and investment as a ratio to GDP has remained reasonably high by historical standards.[23]

---

[21] Adams, Fenton, and Larsen (1987) discuss this issue in more detail.

[22] See the survey of the literature in Adams, Fenton, and Larsen (1987).

[23] For relevant data on this point, see Table 2.3 in Maddison (1991).

III The Expansion and Integration of International Financial Markets

In addition to the shift from a pegged to a mixed exchange rate system, two other key structural changes in the international economy since the collapse of the Bretton Woods system have been the rapid expansion of private international financial markets and the removal of capital account restrictions in the industrial countries.[24] These changes in international financial markets have been reflected in the growing commitment by many countries to current and capital account convertibility, the sharp expansion in the scale of net and gross capital flows in the major industrial countries, the globalization and integration of offshore and major domestic markets, the dominant role of private flows in the financing of fiscal and current account imbalances, the growing importance of institutional investors in cross-border securities transactions, and the sharp increase in the use of derivative financial instruments. This section first reviews the principal structural changes in international financial markets and then briefly considers some policy implications of these structural changes.

Structural Changes in International Financial Markets

The growth of private international financial markets has been accompanied by an ongoing expansion of current and capital account convertibility. In 1975, only about one third of all IMF members had accepted the obligations of Article VIII to allow current account convertibility, whereas by June 1994 over one half had done so, even as IMF membership was growing from 128 to 178 countries. Progress toward capital account convertibility has been more limited, with most members having imposed some restrictions on capital account transactions throughout the postwar period.[25] However, there has recently been a move to capital account liberalization in the industrial countries and some developing countries, as evidenced by the rise in the number of countries without capital account restrictions from 23 in 1975 to 38 in 1993.[26] This development is in part a manifestation of the erosion of the effectiveness of capital controls in many countries.

Capital account convertibility in the industrial countries has facilitated a sharp expansion in the scale of net and gross capital flows between these countries, as well as increased participation by foreign investors and foreign financial institutions in major domestic financial markets. A sharp upswing in the level of net capital flows among the industrial countries was the counterpart of the historically large current account imbalances during the period. Although large current account imbalances were evident during 1973–75 and in 1979–80, net capital flows between the industrial countries expanded most rapidly after 1982. For example, the net capital inflow into the United States rose from an average of $2 billion a year (0.1 percent of GNP) in 1970–72 to an average of $139 billion a year (3 percent of GNP) in 1985–88 before subsiding to $65 billion a year (1¼ percent of GNP) in the early 1990s.

An even more rapid expansion occurred in gross capital flows, reflecting increased cross-border banking transactions and flows of securities, the development of offshore (Eurocurrency) markets, and the entry of foreign financial institutions into domestic markets. For example, the stock of international loans (net of redepositing by banks) rose from $175 billion at the end of December 1973 (5 percent of industrial countries' GNP) to $3.6 trillion at the end of 1993 (19 percent of the industrial countries' GNP).

---

[24]The former development has been described at length in Goldstein, Folkerts-Landau, and others (1993b).

[25]While the Articles of Agreement encourage the establishment of current account convertibility (Article VIII status), they also permit the use of capital controls. Article VI, Section 3, states:

"Members may exercise such controls as are necessary to regulate international capital movements, but no member may exercise these controls in a manner which will restrict payments for current transactions or which will unduly delay transfers of funds and settlement of commitments, except as provided in Article VII, Section 3(b) and in Article XIV, Section 2."

[26]Alesina, Grilli, and Milesi-Ferretti (1994) discuss the determinants and economic impact of capital controls.

III THE EXPANSION AND INTEGRATION OF INTERNATIONAL FINANCIAL MARKETS

These international capital flows were associated with a sharply increased volume of transactions in both spot and derivative foreign exchange markets. Turnover on the three largest spot foreign exchange markets (London, New York, and Tokyo) increased threefold between 1986 and 1992, with global turnover in April 1992 estimated to be about $880 billion daily. By way of comparison, total non-gold foreign exchange reserves of the industrial countries' central banks amounted to roughly $414 billion at the end of 1993.

The presence of foreign investors in major domestic financial markets also increased as the need to finance large fiscal and current account imbalances in the industrial countries created incentives for removing restrictions on domestic and external financial transactions. While data on the residency of holders of industrial countries' bonds are notoriously poor, the share of public debt of the major industrial countries held by nonresidents exceeded 20 percent in 1993 and appears to be rising. In Germany, for example, central government debt held by foreigners increased from 5 percent at the end of 1974 to 39 percent at the end of 1992.

More generally, while private capital flows played only a limited role in financing fiscal and current account imbalances in the 1950s and 1960s, these flows provided most of the cross-border financing of the imbalances for industrial countries throughout the period since 1970, and for developing countries in the 1970s.[27] The ability of international financial markets to respond to the financing needs associated with adjustments to unanticipated shocks was demonstrated in the early 1990s following the reunification of Germany. In the three years prior to German reunification, Germany was a net exporter of capital to the rest of the world, with a current account surplus of about $50 billion per annum. Following the reunification, the German current account balance switched to deficits of $20 billion in 1991, $26 billion in 1992, and $22 billion in 1993. Although Germany's foreign direct investment abroad declined, the current account deficit was financed principally by sharp increases in inflows of portfolio investment and to the banking sector.

Although many developing countries lost access to international financial markets during the 1980s, the renewed access of developing countries to these markets has been evident in the sharp increase in capital flows to developing countries in the early 1990s. Between 1990 and 1993, net private capital flows to developing countries are estimated to have risen from $43 billion to $113 billion, and, in 1992–93, these flows were larger than official flows for the first time in a decade.[28] Since the 1970s, the source of these flows has shifted from banks to nonbanks in the form of bonds, equity portfolio investment, and foreign direct investment; meanwhile, inflows have shifted from predominantly sovereign to mainly private borrowers, with flows between private market participants now accounting for almost 60 percent of the net flows. However, most of these inflows were to middle-income countries that had either avoided commercial bank debt-servicing difficulties in the 1980s or successfully resolved such earlier problems. Apart from China and India, most low-income countries have not participated in these inflows, and they continue to rely heavily on official financing.

Another aspect of the structural changes in international financial markets has been the growing importance of institutional investors in cross-border capital flows, especially in securities transactions. In the early 1970s, large institutional investors, such as pension funds, insurance companies, and mutual funds, played only a limited role in cross-border capital flows, owing to both official restrictions and the high costs of acquiring and managing diversified international portfolios. In the 1980s, however, the role of institutional investors in channeling funds between savers and investors increased, reflecting the lower transactions costs for institutional investors relative to individual investors, the increased willingness of individual savers to allow their portfolios to be managed by agents, and, in some countries, the tax advantages enjoyed by contractual savings plans.

The asset price variability that characterized international financial markets in the 1980s and early 1990s has also stimulated the use of a variety of over-the-counter and exchange-traded derivative instruments (mainly futures, options, and swaps). For example, at the end of 1992, the principal value of outstanding interest rate and currency swaps was $5.6 trillion, five times the value at the end of 1987. More generally, the principal amount of exchange-traded derivative instruments increased by 69 percent in 1993, reaching $7.8 trillion, which was more than 12 times the total in 1986.[29]

Policy Implications of Structural Changes in International Financial Markets

The expansion of international financial markets and the movement toward current and capital

---

[27] For example, when the United States ran a cumulative current account deficit of $664 billion between 1983 and 1988, inflows of portfolio investment, other private short-term capital, and net foreign direct investment financed about 75 percent of the external deficit.

[28] This net capital flow includes net bonds issued on international capital markets, commercial bank lending, foreign direct investment, other private flows, and portfolio equity flows.

[29] A more detailed discussion of derivative markets can be found in Goldstein, Folkerts-Landau, and others (1993b).

account convertibility have influenced the distribution of global savings and investment, the formulation and disciplining of macroeconomic policies, the coordination of supervisory and regulatory policies, and the structure of the international reserve system.

The structural changes that have occurred in international capital markets since the collapse of the Bretton Woods system have clearly increased the international linkages between major domestic and offshore financial markets, particularly in the industrial countries. The capital markets of developing countries are also becoming more closely integrated with markets in the rest of the world, although they have progressed far less in that direction than industrial countries. It is still premature to speak of a single, global capital market where most of the world's savings are auctioned to the highest bidder and where a wide range of assets carry the same risk-adjusted return. However, access to international financial markets has become an increasingly important determinant of the share of global savings that is likely to accrue to a particular country.

Experience since the debt crisis has demonstrated that creditworthiness considerations play a dominant role in determining both the cost and availability of credit from international financial markets. While there is considerable debate about how well the markets evaluate the willingness and the ability of borrowers to service their debt obligations, it is clear that the perception that a borrower's creditworthiness has deteriorated or is about to deteriorate can lead to an abrupt curtailment of funding, which may be difficult—even in the medium term—to reverse. The evaluation of a country's creditworthiness is done on a continuing basis and is influenced by the market participants' perception of the quality of a country's macroeconomic and financial policies. Creditworthiness is evaluated most explicitly by credit-rating agencies, which characterize the investment quality of a country's external debt.

These tighter connections between access to major domestic and offshore financial markets and the market's evaluation of a country's policies have reduced in some respects the authorities' autonomy in conducting macroeconomic policies. It has become difficult to resist private markets when they have reached the concerted view that the outlook for a particular security or currency has changed. Thus, perceptions that a country is following weak or inconsistent policies can have an immediate impact on not only its cost of funds and access to international credit but also its ability to sustain a particular exchange rate or monetary policy.

With the benefit of hindsight, it is not difficult to identify instances over the past two decades when participants in international capital markets may not have paid enough attention to the economic fundamentals. The buildup to the external debt crisis in the 1970s, the run-up of the U.S. dollar in 1984–85, and the large shift of funds into EMS countries with higher interest rates in the late 1980s provide some examples.[30] Nonetheless, it is difficult to conclude that private capital markets usually "got it wrong" in deciding which securities and currencies were worthwhile investments and which ones were not. If there is a problem with the operation of international capital markets, it is often that the verdict of the marketplace comes late in the day, and then with a vengeance. For all concerned, it would be better if the adjustment to changing perceptions regarding economic prospects occurred earlier and in a more orderly and consistent manner.

As for the implications for the exchange rate regime of this increased market discipline, it would be too extreme to assert that the growth and agility of private financial markets now make it unrealistic to operate fixed exchange rate arrangements. Nonetheless, the growth of these markets has made the conditions for maintaining a fixed exchange rate system more demanding. In particular, there is now less room for divergence of views among participants about the appropriate stance and medium-term orientation of monetary policy, less time to adjust to large, country-specific shocks, and greater pressure to achieve closer convergence of economic performance. Nonetheless, some countries will find that it is in their interest to participate in fixed exchange rate arrangements, and that they can credibly commit to those requirements.

The growing influence of private markets on the sustainability of macroeconomic policies provides a case for trying to improve the consistency and effectiveness of market discipline. Two considerations seem particularly important. First, market participants must have a full understanding of a debtor's obligations if they are to accurately assess its debt-servicing obligations and capacity. The more limited that information, the more likely it is that "contagion effects" will be present, as it could prove difficult to distinguish better credit risks from weaker ones. Better disclosure requirements and harmonization of accounting standards across countries would be particularly helpful. Second, the discipline exercised by the market will be weakened if the participants believe that the borrower will be bailed out in the event of an actual or impending default. If such a perception exists, the interest rate paid by the borrower will reflect the creditworthiness of the per-

---

[30]For a description of this last development, see Chapter III, "Prologue to the ERM Crisis: 'Convergence Play'," in Goldstein, Folkerts-Landau, and others (1993a).

III THE EXPANSION AND INTEGRATION OF INTERNATIONAL FINANCIAL MARKETS

ceived guarantor, and there will be little incentive for either the borrower to curb its activities, or the lender to monitor the borrower's activities. However, it may be very difficult to make a "no-bailout" pledge credible, especially if it is perceived that there would be large systemic repercussions associated with a particular failure.

While financial innovations and the ongoing internationalization of financial activities have been sources of major efficiency gains, they also have exposed gaps in supervisory and regulatory regimes and put new pressures on payments, clearance, and settlement systems. In the foreign exchange markets, for example, such gaps were first evident in 1974 when the failure of Bankhaus Herstatt and Franklin National Bank indicated the scale of losses that could be associated with open positions in foreign exchange markets and settlement failures.

To reduce the systemic risk that large institutional failures in one market can immediately have on institutions in a broad range of other markets, there has been a concerted effort over the past two decades to improve the international coordination of supervisory and regulatory policies.[31] These efforts have focused on coordinating on an international level the strengthening of the capital base of banks and securities firms; assigning supervisory responsibility for the foreign branches and subsidiaries of banks and securities houses; harmonizing reporting and disclosure requirements; and developing measures to strengthen major payments, clearance, and settlement systems. These efforts have resulted in the development of risk-weighted capital-adequacy standards for international banks by the Basle Committee on Banking Supervision and the Basle Concordat of 1975, which assigned responsibility for the supervision of foreign branches, subsidiaries, and joint ventures.[32] In addition, the Committee has also generated discussions of minimum capital-adequacy standards for securities firms within the context of the Technical Committee of the International Organization of Securities Commissions, of improvements in interbank netting arrangements in offshore payments systems, and of the harmonization of clearance and settlement arrangements in industrial countries and some developing countries.

---

[31]The general nature of the systemic risks in international financial markets has been addressed more fully in Goldstein, Folkerts-Landau, and others (1994).

[32]The Concordat was subsequently revised in 1978, 1983, and 1990 to provide for a consolidated supervision, inclusive of foreign branches and subsidiaries, of banks' capital adequacy and the supervision of banks' holding companies, and to improve the flow of information among supervisors. The problems associated with the implementation of the Concordat are discussed in El-Erian (1992).

Despite the shift to more flexible exchange rates following the collapse of the Bretton Woods system, countries have continued to increase their holdings of international reserves. Reserves are held as a precaution against unanticipated shocks, for foreign exchange market intervention, and as a means of demonstrating creditworthiness. As private international financial markets have expanded, many countries have acquired reserves by borrowing on international markets. For countries without access to capital markets, reserves have had to be obtained by improving their current account position, which has required a compression of domestic demand relative to production in order to reduce net imports. While a loss of market access has often reflected unsound macroeconomic policies, the restoration of such access can take considerable time, even following the implementation of stabilization programs.

For countries with access to international financial markets, borrowed reserves have provided a flexible and efficient means of adjusting their gross reserve positions. However, the net cost of holding borrowed reserves—the excess of the cost of borrowed funds over the return earned on reserve assets—is significant for all but the major reserve-currency countries, and the cost is particularly large for many of the poorer countries in the world. While this risk premium may be appropriate in many circumstances, it is not clear that it is justified in cases in which reserves are not drawn down permanently but are held in order to provide short-term macroeconomic flexibility for the countries concerned. Nonetheless, many countries have generally considered it desirable to incur the carrying costs of reserves rather than rely on their ability to obtain credit during periods of need, partly because this access to financial markets is often restricted at the very time when they need foreign financing. However, many developing countries and countries in transition have very low levels of reserves relative to plausible standards of reserve needs.

These changes in access to financial markets and the cost of foreign funds highlight some potential disadvantages of a reserve system heavily dependent on borrowed reserves. In part, the potential role of the SDR in meeting the long-term global need for supplementing reserves depends upon whether international financial markets are likely to be an efficient and reliable source of borrowed reserves over time.[33] In this connection, it is argued that SDR allocations could reduce the vulnerability of the reserve system to disturbances in financial

---

[33]For a more extensive discussion of the role of the SDR in the international monetary system, see International Monetary Fund (1987). For an analysis of why the SDR has so far not played a key role in the international monetary system, see Rhomberg (1991).

markets by providing countries with sufficient stocks of owned reserves that would be available during a crisis. Furthermore, because the costs of increasing reserve holdings through borrowing or net import compression are, for most countries, significantly higher than the true economic opportunity cost to the world of creating additional reserves through SDR allocation, there could be other advantages to a reserve system that relied more heavily on the SDR.[34] More generally, it can be argued that there is presently evidence of a long-term global need for reserve supplementation and that, given such a global need, the objectives specified in the Article of Agreement provide a plausible case for allocating a moderate amount of SDRs.

Other considerations, however, can be cited as indicating that there may not be a long-term global need for supplementing reserves in the form of SDRs. First, it would appear that many of the countries that account for the bulk of world trade are not facing difficulties in satisfying their growing demand for reserve assets. Indeed, the rising ratio of nongold reserves to imports in many developing countries can be interpreted as indicating that the reserve-creation mechanism is not acting abnormally. Finally, the low reserves of many developing countries may, in fact, reflect inadequate or inappropriate macroeconomic and financial policies. In these countries, there is a need for policy adjustments supported by conditional lending, and unconditional reserves provided by an SDR allocation might well be spent, resulting in a permanent transfer of resources.

---

[34]The differentials that countries face between borrowing costs on private capital markets and rates of return on reserve holdings are generally regarded as premiums that private lenders require to compensate for the risk that borrowers will not comply fully with the terms of loan contracts. The cost saving that takes place when reserves are acquired through SDR allocations rather than borrowing points to the absence of a risk premium in the SDR system, which is reflected in the fact that the rate of charge that is levied against a country's cumulative allocation of SDRs is identical to the rate of interest that is paid on a country's holdings of SDRs. The absence of a spread between the two rates would create the potential for undesired resource transfers if it were risky to hold SDRs. For a discussion of the issue of resource transfers and the SDR system, see Coats, Furstenberg, and Isard (1990).

IV Volatility, Misalignment, and Access to Capital

As described in the preceding two sections, the hallmark of the current international monetary system is diversity, both in exchange rate arrangements and the functioning of financial markets. This diversity contrasts with the Bretton Woods system of par values for exchange rates—an arrangement made possible in part by relatively limited international financial flows, supplemented on occasion by capital controls. The maintenance of pegged exchange rates in the face of external imbalances was achieved partly through the use of official reserve assets. The post-Bretton Woods exchange and payments environment is much more flexible, and the options available for dealing with external imbalances have expanded in two fundamental ways. For many countries, adjustment is achieved largely through continuous market-determined changes in exchange rates, while the remaining imbalances are typically financed by private capital markets, at least for most industrial and now many developing countries.

The flexibility made possible by the availability of these options has enabled the international monetary system to adjust fairly smoothly to a wide array of shocks, such as the oil price hikes of 1973 and 1979; it is far from obvious that these shocks would have been absorbed as easily under a par value system. While the flexibility provided by the floating exchange rate system and open capital markets has generally been beneficial, it is not clear that it has always been well used by policymakers. Floating exchange rates have on occasion been associated with unwise monetary policies and high inflation, and the breadth and depth of financial markets may have allowed some policymakers to implement less prudent fiscal policies than would have been possible under the Bretton Woods system. This underlines the need for effective surveillance of economic policies by the IMF.

As discussed above, one form of surveillance is provided by private investors in financial markets. In principle, the response of private markets can be highly beneficial in disciplining government behavior. However, the discipline exercised by investors in these markets is neither infallible nor always applied smoothly and consistently.

With respect to exchange rates, there is concern that private markets may not always anchor their behavior to economic fundamentals, thus making their responses susceptible to contagion and bandwagon effects that may be disruptive and detrimental to economic performance. These concerns tend to focus on two areas. First, the volatility of floating exchange rates between countries could result in economic disruption, thereby reducing the volume of international trade and perhaps investment. Second, exchange rate misalignments, such as the episode of the U.S. dollar in the mid-1980s, can lead to a misallocation of resources and major adjustment problems.

Finally, the abrupt cessation of access to private capital markets experienced by many developing countries during the debt crisis of the early 1980s, as well as the size of private capital flows into many developing countries in the early 1990s, has also produced concern about the consistency with which private capital markets make such funds available. This aspect of international capital markets is discussed in the last part of this section.

Volatility

Chart 2 illustrates the dramatic change in the variability of nominal exchange rates across the major currencies after the breakdown of the Bretton Woods fixed exchange rate system. The three panels show monthly changes in nominal exchange rates between the currencies of the three largest industrial countries since 1962. In the 1960s, monthly variations in bilateral exchange rates were negligible, as would be expected, but after 1973 these monthly changes became much larger and less predictable. This volatility in nominal exchange rates was reflected in higher volatility of real exchange rates and, hence, in greater uncertainty.

Furthermore, despite the evolution of the international monetary system since 1973, particularly with regard to capital markets, no significant trend in the underlying levels of volatility in these

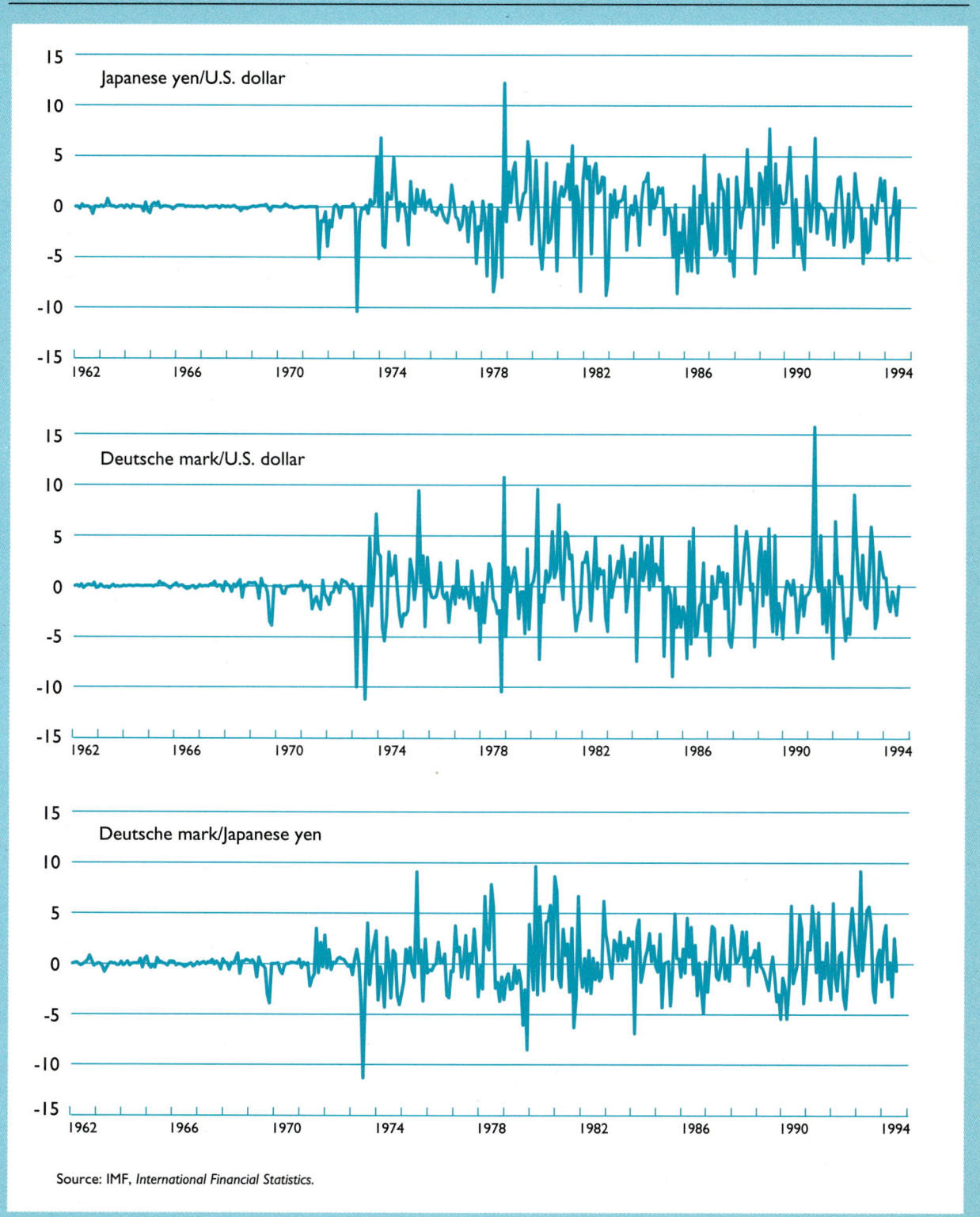

Chart 2. Germany, Japan, and the United States: Volatility of Nominal Exchange Rates, January 1962–July 1994
(Percent changes from previous month)

Source: IMF, *International Financial Statistics*.

IV VOLATILITY, MISALIGNMENT, AND ACCESS TO CAPITAL

exchange rates has emerged over time, although markets do appear to go through identifiable phases of relative calm and turbulence. This pattern is not unique to foreign exchange markets. Indeed, it appears to be a very general feature of asset markets that are not subject to limits on price changes, as similar erratic short-term price movements are evident in stock and bond markets, and in earlier periods of floating exchange rates.

To some extent, this volatility reflects the forward-looking nature of asset markets in general, and foreign exchange markets in particular. Market prices are continuously updated as news about the future becomes available. As this news is, by definition, unpredictable, so are the movements in market prices. This situation implies that a certain level of unpredictability is probably an inevitable characteristic of unconstrained exchange markets. However, this does not necessarily imply that all of the volatility that is observed is beneficial. There is evidence that the behavior of many participants in these markets is not based solely on fundamentals but depends upon "psychological factors" and public opinion, and there is an expanding literature on how this type of behavior can increase underlying price volatility.[35]

It is also clear that bilateral exchange rate volatility can be reduced by government policies, even in a system of floating exchange rates between the main industrial countries. Chart 3 shows the monthly movements between the Canadian and U.S. dollars, and between the deutsche mark and the currencies of two of Germany's main European trading partners, the French franc and the pound sterling. The Canadian dollar shows significantly lower volatility than the yen or deutsche mark against the U.S. dollar, presumably reflecting, at least in part, the desire of the Canadian authorities to reduce erratic movements in the exchange rate.[36] The behavior of the deutsche mark with respect to the French franc, particularly after 1987, illustrates the effect of membership in a fixed exchange rate system (the ERM) on the volatility of bilateral exchange rates. During the 1980s, the variability of the French franc with respect to the deutsche mark was clearly lower than that experienced between the deutsche mark and the pound sterling, or between the deutsche mark and the French franc in the 1970s.[37] The Netherlands guilder, as shown in Table 2, exhibits an even lower level of exchange rate variability in the ERM. Indeed, in this case, the variability in its real exchange rate over the 1980s has been considerably lower than under the Bretton Woods fixed exchange rate system.

The concern raised by high levels of nominal exchange rate volatility is that it engenders greater uncertainty about relative prices, which, in turn, generates lower levels of international trade, investment, and confidence. The fear that floating rates would be unstable and would have adverse effects on the volume of international transactions was a factor inhibiting the shift away from the Bretton Woods system. Certainly, greater nominal exchange rate volatility has produced greater variability in real exchange rates.[38] As can be seen in Table 2, the standard deviation of month-to-month changes in the real exchange rate between the U.S. dollar, the yen, and the deutsche mark since 1973 has risen over threefold, from under 1 percent per annum prior to 1972 to over 3 percent subsequently, while the volatility of exchange rates between the Canadian and U.S. dollars, the Swiss franc and the deutsche mark, and the pound sterling and the deutsche mark has doubled. At the same time, however, the development of liquid derivative markets in foreign exchange futures and options, which provide vehicles for hedging the risks generated by exchange rate volatility, has partially mitigated the importance of this higher volatility.

The increase in exchange rate volatility after 1973 has generated a large number of studies of the effect on trade, using time series, cross-section, and survey techniques. Much of this work has started from existing empirical models of trade volumes, which explain trade relatively successfully by using levels of real exchange rates and activity. The impact of exchange rate volatility is then measured by adding a term representing this volatility into the equation. While estimates have varied, the overall consensus in the literature is that the negative effects of higher exchange rate volatility on trade is small.[39] For example, a recent paper (Frankel and Wei, 1993), which used a particularly large set of data on bilateral trade between 63 countries, found that while exchange rate volatility had a significant impact on trade, a doubling of the level of real exchange rate variability in Europe in 1990 (which would have returned such variability to its 1980, pre-ERM value), would have lowered intra-regional trade volumes by only 0.7 percent.

The literature on the relationship between exchange rate volatility and investment is considerably smaller than that on trade and exchange rate

---

[35] Group of Ten Deputies (1993) and Shleifer and Summers (1990).

[36] The behavior of the Swiss franc with respect to the deutsche mark shows a similar pattern (Table 2).

[37] The pound sterling did not join the ERM until October 1990.

[38] This is also true for the interwar period, as discussed in Eichengreen (1988).

[39] See IMF (1984a) for a survey, and Commission of the European Communities (1990) and Gagnon (1993) for a discussion of more recent results.

Chart 3. Volatility of Selected Nominal Exchange Rates, January 1962–July 1994
(Percent changes from previous month)

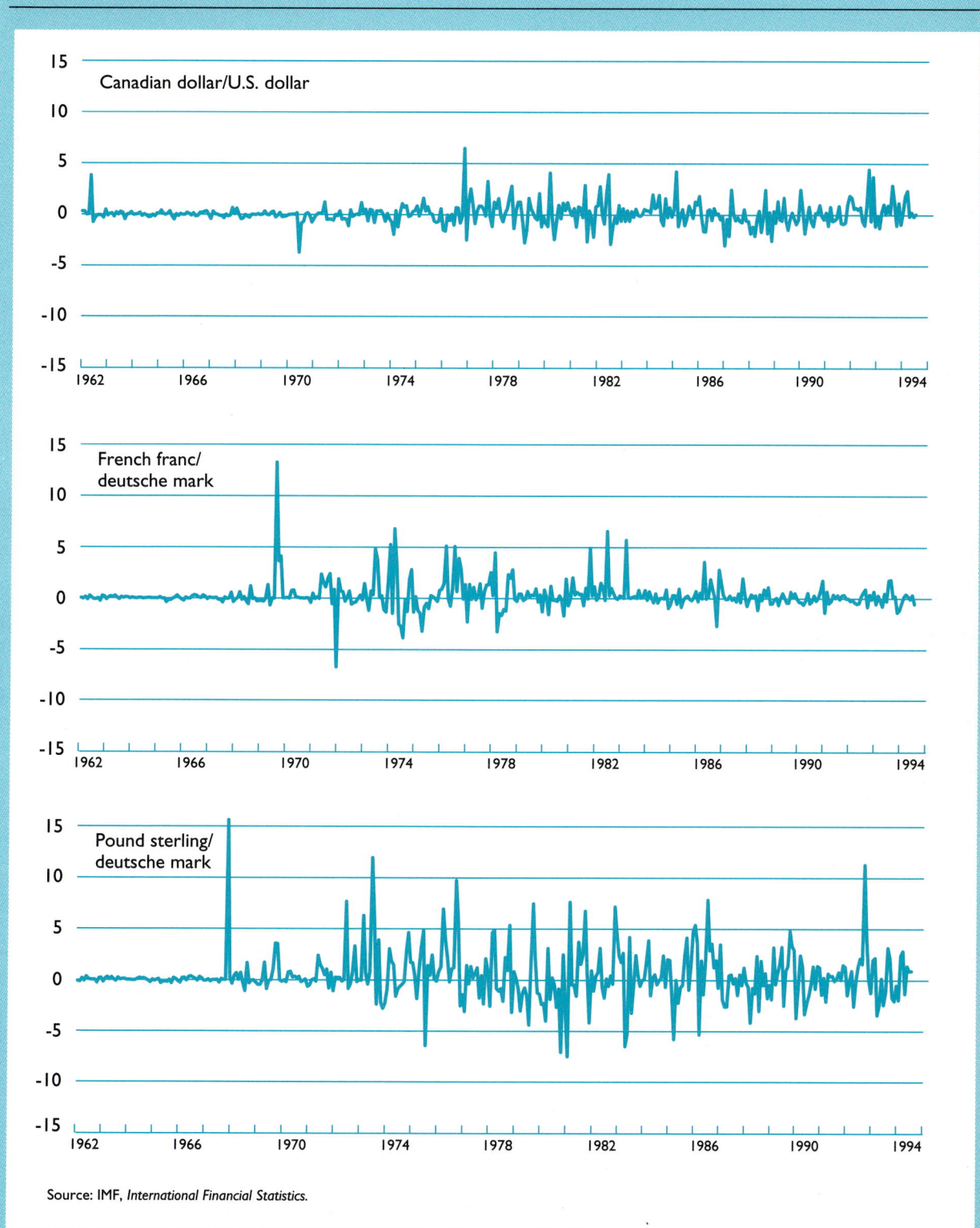

Source: IMF, *International Financial Statistics*.

IV VOLATILITY, MISALIGNMENT, AND ACCESS TO CAPITAL

volatility. However, the work that does exist appears to come to a very similar conclusion, namely, that the effect is small.[40] Others have argued that higher exchange rate volatility could adversely affect the efficiency of the economic system more generally by reducing the information content in relative prices.[41] However, this connection also has little hard empirical support. While the coincidence between the advent of the floating exchange rate regime and the slowdown in economic growth in many regions of the world after 1973 suggests some kind of relationship, there is little firm evidence that volatility stemming from floating exchange rates has had a significant impact on the slowdown in growth. Similarly, it does not appear that floating exchange rates have inhibited economic integration. Canada and the United States, as well as Switzerland and Germany, continue to maintain close economic ties despite floating bilateral exchange rates, albeit with somewhat lower volatility than is observed between the major currencies (Table 2).

However, many private businesses whose success is strongly linked to international trade see exchange rate volatility as a matter of serious concern. Many of these foreign exchange risks can be hedged through an increasingly elaborate array of financial market instruments, but such hedging is generally not without costs. In the aggregate, the real economic risks associated with uncertainty concerning the behavior of real exchange rates must be borne by someone; and the bearers of such risks must generally be paid an adequate return to give them an incentive to provide this service.

Moreover, it is clear that many governments, particularly in Europe, are concerned about the possible negative effects of exchange rate volatility on their economies. One explanation for this difference in perception is the very fast pace and high level of economic integration within the EU.[42] While exchange rate volatility may not be a significant impediment to a relatively gradual trend toward integration, as exemplified by the United States and Canada, it may be more disruptive when economies are integrating as rapidly as has been the case in the EU over the past two decades, and as is projected to continue with the establishment of the single European Market and, ultimately, monetary union.

The costs of exchange rate volatility have to be weighed against the benefits provided by floating exchange rates, in particular the ability to direct macroeconomic policy toward domestic objectives. Any sustained reduction in exchange rate volatility involves a decision to orient macroeconomic policies more toward influencing the behavior of the exchange rate. The authorities in the three largest industrial economies appear to have reached the judgment that, in light of their limited trade linkages with each other and relatively asymmetric underlying disturbances, the benefits provided by stabilizing exchange rates between these three currencies are outweighed by the potential losses that would result from less flexible domestic policies.[43] The literature on optimum currency areas supports this view.[44] However, other countries with greater trade links, less diverse disturbances, and explicit and concrete economic integration objectives may well reach a different conclusion. Indeed, one of the three major industrial countries—Germany—has very close trading links with other European countries and therefore participates in the ERM.

Exchange Rate Misalignments

A second concern with floating exchange rates is that they have been prone to generate misalignments in exchange rates. Such misalignments can arise when an exchange rate moves away from the level consistent with economic fundamentals for a prolonged period of time, or when an exchange rate reflects policies that are inappropriate and unsustainable. The most striking, and most generally acknowledged, example of a misalignment is the 50 percent real appreciation of the U.S. dollar between 1980 and early 1985 (Chart 1). As discussed above, however, there are several other examples of large changes in real exchange rates over relatively short periods, such as the appreciation of the yen in 1978, of the pound sterling in the early 1980s, and, more recently, of the yen since early 1993.

---

[40] Goldberg (1993) provides some empirical estimates of the effects of exchange rate volatility on U.S. investment. Aizenman (1992) examines in a theoretical model the implications of exchange rate flexibility for domestic and foreign investment.

[41] For example, see Krugman (1989).

[42] Commission of the European Communities (1990) has suggested another explanation, namely, that despite having a small impact on trade, floating exchange rates could have a considerable impact on the welfare of those who engage in trade if trading is very profitable.

[43] This does not mean that it is never appropriate to pursue specific exchange rate objectives, as illustrated by the Plaza Agreement and the Louvre Accord. However, formal exchange rate targets for the currencies of these countries are unlikely to be beneficial. This remains true for Japan and the United States, even though they have relatively large bilateral trade links, because the overall importance of international trade is comparatively small in both countries.

[44] Part II of Goldstein and others (1992), "Issues in the Operation of Monetary Unions and Common Currency Areas," provides a survey of the relevant literature and arguments. Bayoumi and Eichengreen (1994) discuss the correlation of disturbances across the major industrial countries in relation to other regions of the world.

Unlike volatility, the economic harm that can be caused by exchange rate misalignments is relatively clear. As illustrated in Chart 4, U.S. real exports stagnated in the mid-1980s under the impact of the strong dollar, and many tradable goods industries suffered considerable economic disruption. The subsequent fall in the dollar led, with a lag, to a revival in U.S. real exports. Exchange rate misalignments, particularly between the major currencies, can also have costs for other nations. As already noted, one of the reasons for the decline in the use of fixed parities by developing countries was the instability in the relative values of the major currencies. Finally, misalignments that result in exchange rate appreciations are also costly in that they can generate protectionist measures. Such concerns about protectionist pressures arising from the misalignment of the dollar in 1984–85 were highlighted in the Plaza Agreement.

In discussing exchange rate misalignments, it is useful to distinguish between those exchange rate changes that reflect government policies or other underlying disturbances and those that appear to reflect pure bandwagon effects. For example, at least part of the appreciation of the U.S. dollar in the early 1980s was due to the combination of a relatively expansionary fiscal policy and a contractionary monetary policy.[45] If the exchange rate only reflected such fundamentals as monetary and fiscal policies, these misalignments would reflect the inappropriate choice of domestic policies. While this might well be a cause for concern, such misalignments would not be a criticism of the international monetary system as such, except to the extent that the exchange rate regime itself might make the choice of such policies easier.

Movements in exchange rates, however, do not seem to be always closely connected with changes in economic fundamentals. For example, the final stage in the appreciation of the U.S. dollar in late 1984 and early 1985 appeared at the time, and still appears, to have gone beyond what could have been justified by the fundamentals. Similar concerns have been raised about other large movements in exchange rates that seem to be unrelated to underlying exchange rate determinants, such as the appreciation of sterling in 1979–81 and the more recent appreciation of the yen. Unfortunately, because there is no precise or reliable connection between exchange rates and their economic determinants, it is not always possible to make a clear distinction between exchange rate movements that correspond to fundamentals and

Chart 4. United States: Real Exports and Imports of Goods and Services, January 1973–June 1994
(In percent of real GDP)

Source: U.S. Bureau of Economic Analysis, National Income and Product Accounts.

those that do not.[46] Hence, it is difficult to identify occasions on which intervention might be warranted or to put an estimate on the costs to the international economy from bandwagon effects in exchange rate markets.[47]

From the point of view of the appropriate macroeconomic policy response, it is useful to make a distinction between misalignments that result in a depreciation of the exchange rate and those that involve an appreciation. Persistent downward pressure on exchange rates, such as occurred to the U.S. dollar, the pound sterling, and the Italian lira at various times in the mid-to-late 1970s, generally reflect the pursuit of undesirable economic policies. In such cases, the nature of the required policy adjustment is generally clear and noncontroversial, namely, a tightening of monetary and fiscal policies in those countries whose currencies are depreciating. When the misalignment involves an exchange rate appreciation, however, the appropriate policy response is typically less transparent. Depending on the situation with respect to inflation, it might be

---

[45] Similarly, the appreciation of the pound sterling in the early 1980s was attributable, at least in part, to the combination of increasing production of North Sea oil and the tight monetary policy of the government.

[46] Clark and others (1994) provide a discussion of the relationship between exchange rates and fundamentals. Estimates reported in Barrell and Wren-Lewis (1989) of fundamental exchange rates, defined as the exchange rate consistent with external and internal balance, indicate several large misalignments during the 1980s.

[47] It is important to note that the movements of the U.S. dollar and the pound sterling both occurred at times when the authorities were following an explicit policy of not interfering with the market-determined value of their respective currencies.

IV VOLATILITY, MISALIGNMENT, AND ACCESS TO CAPITAL

inadvisable to ease the monetary stance significantly by lowering interest rates. The implications for the fiscal policy stance are not clear, as fiscal consolidation could actually strengthen the exchange rate through its impact on inflationary expectations, whereas a fiscal expansion could run counter to the appropriate medium-term fiscal objectives. Misalignments involving highly appreciated exchange rates may therefore pose more difficulties for policymakers than those associated with depreciated rates.

Problems arising from exchange rate misalignments are not limited to floating exchange rate regimes. If the concern with floating exchange rates is that nominal exchange rates can move too much, the concern with fixed but adjustable exchange rate regimes is that they move too little, partly because changing the parity is often viewed as an admission of economic failure. One of the problems in the late 1960s was the unwillingness of U.S. policymakers to consider a devaluation of the dollar in terms of gold. Similarly, some of the more recent problems of the ERM may have stemmed, at least in part, from an unwillingness to realign parities in the face of both the macroeconomic effects of German unification and the steady real appreciation of some currencies, most notably the lira, which was caused by the consistently higher inflation rate in Italy relative to Germany.

These twin concerns, namely, that fixed exchange rate regimes are too rigid, while floating rate regimes exhibit exchange rate movements that are too large, have led some commentators on the international monetary system (most notably John Williamson) to advocate the establishment of target zones for the major exchange rates.[48] Such zones, it is argued, would be wide enough to provide flexibility in the face of disturbances but narrow enough to avoid significant misalignments of real exchange rates. Some issues associated with implementing such a proposal are discussed in Section V below.

Access to International Capital Markets

A third concern with the current international financial system is that, while international capital markets are wider and deeper than at any point in the postwar period, access to these capital markets, particularly by less developed countries, is erratic. In particular, the international debt crisis, sparked by the problems of Mexico in 1982, is widely regarded as having lowered market access for many countries whose underlying performance remained satisfactory. Similarly, there remains a suspicion that the current enthusiasm for investing in many of the developing countries may result in the granting of imprudent loans, as happened before the onset of the debt crisis in the 1970s.

Nor is this boom-and-bust cycle in international capital markets unique to the postwar period. The nineteenth century saw a succession of such cycles in international lending, during which the availability of international capital fluctuated substantially.[49] These patterns appear to be a characteristic of private capital markets that is similar, at least in some respects, to volatility in asset prices, which has already been discussed. Indeed, private capital markets tend to focus primarily on the issue of creditworthiness, that is, on the possibility that the credit that has been extended may not be promptly or fully repaid. Sharp and sudden discipline is imposed in the form of a credit cutoff when the market becomes persuaded that the risk of nonrepayment has become significant. The private credit market, however, sometimes exhibits little concern about the use of credit or the level and extent of borrowing up to the point that the borrower's creditworthiness comes into question. Thus, it would be imprudent to rely exclusively on private credit markets to exercise surveillance of economic policy and performance on a continuous and timely basis.

Changes in access to international capital can be costly. The debt crisis caused severe economic disruption in large parts of the developing world, as lack of access to international capital markets limited economic policy options, constrained trade, and generated economic and political instability. Furthermore, these problems were clearly exacerbated by the high levels of debt that many developing countries were able to issue during the 1970s. The difficulty of obtaining access to international credit markets is particularly acute for many of the poorer nations in the world, and for the economies in transition, some of which lack the resources to secure private loans for basic requirements, such as adequate levels of reserves. Unfortunately, there are no simple remedies to these problems of erratic access. Some of the issues involved are discussed in Section VI below.[50]

---

[48] Williamson (1985) and Williamson and Miller (1987).

[49] Williamson (1985) and Fishlow (1985) provide a discussion of these developments.

[50] See also Schadler and others (1993) for a discussion of recent surges in capital flows to developing countries.

V Limiting Exchange Rate Variability: The Target Zone Method

As long as the exchange rates between the currencies of the major industrial countries continue to fluctuate widely, either for reasons that are not clearly linked to changes in economic fundamentals or on account of inappropriate policies, suggestions for a fundamental reform of the system aimed at diminishing these exchange rate fluctuations are likely to continue to be proposed. These proposals often call for the establishment of target zones for the bilateral exchange rates of the three largest industrial countries, with the aim of reducing exchange rate volatility and the probability of exchange rate misalignments while retaining a significant level of flexibility for domestic policies.[51] More generally, advocates of target zones seek to move the present international monetary system in the direction of greater centralization and more explicit cooperation and coordination of economic policies, in order to prevent the exchange rates of the three largest industrial countries from fluctuating to the extent that has been recorded since the end of the Bretton Woods system. Underlying these proposals is the view that the revealed preference of Germany, Japan, and the United States for a system of managed floating is not conducive to the proper functioning of the international monetary system. With target zones, it is argued, an explicit structure of specific exchange rate arrangements will lead to both better exchange rate behavior and more disciplined and appropriate economic policies on the part of the three largest industrial economies.

The distinction between a system of target zones and the present system of managed floating between the three most important currencies is a matter of degree. A "quiet" or "soft" system of target zones—with wide and unannounced exchange rate ranges, limited commitments to intervene to defend these zones, and no firm understandings and little willingness to adjust monetary policies for exchange rate purposes—could be little different from the present system of policy coordination among the major countries. It would be a mistake to characterize the formalization of such a weak system of target zones as a "fundamental reform" of the international monetary system or to expect that it would accomplish something significantly different from the present system. Accordingly, to provide a meaningful contrast between the proposals for fundamental reform and evolutionary improvement of the international monetary system, it is useful to define three characteristics of a target zone system that would clearly distinguish it from the present system. First, the permitted ranges for exchange rates, together with the mechanisms for adjusting these ranges, should imply notably smaller fluctuations between the exchange rates of the major currencies than has been observed in recent years. Second, relatively firm commitments should be made to intervene in substantial amounts to defend the agreed ranges for exchange rates. Third, although domestic monetary policies would retain considerable independence and the commitments to defend exchange rate zones would not be absolute, it should clearly be understood that monetary policies would sometimes need to be adjusted for exchange rate purposes, even when this might be inconvenient from the perspective of the key domestic objectives of monetary policy.

Benefits and Costs of Target Zones

Supporters of target zones make a number of arguments as to why the establishment of these zones would improve the functioning of the exchange rate system. First, target zones would impose more discipline on macroeconomic policies in two ways: to maintain exchange rates within the zones, monetary policy—and sometimes also fiscal policy—would need to be adjusted; and, if the authorities opted to alter the zone rather than their policies, they would need to explain why a new zone was appropriate and convince other participants accordingly. The latter requirement would be likely to strengthen the element of peer pressure in the policy formulation process.

---

[51] Target zones have been proposed for some time by Williamson; see Williamson (1985), Williamson and Miller (1987), and Williamson and Henning (1994). For a discussion and analysis of many of the issues related to target zones, see Frenkel and Goldstein (1986).

V LIMITING EXCHANGE RATE VARIABILITY: THE TARGET ZONE METHOD

Second, target zones are said to improve the international consistency of macroeconomic policies. These zones would have to be negotiated and would therefore require a mutual consistency among exchange rates. It is argued that the exchange rate implications of alternative stances and mixes of macroeconomic policies would thus have to be dealt with directly. In a related vein, supporters argue that the negotiation and revision of target zones could act as a convenient organizing framework for multilateral surveillance.

Third, by promoting greater exchange rate stability, target zones are viewed as providing an anchor for medium-term exchange rate expectations. The peer pressure to keep the exchange rate within the zone would give market participants useful information about the future course of monetary policy, thereby lessening the danger that short-term deviations of policy would be erroneously extrapolated into the future.

Fourth, because the members of a target zone system would be the key-currency industrial countries, it is claimed that target zones would reduce the asymmetry in adjustment in the present exchange rate system. In particular, it would subject the countries whose policies have the greatest spillover effects on the world economy to the same scrutiny and pressure experienced by smaller countries with external and internal imbalances.

In addition to the benefits deriving from discipline and cooperation, proponents have argued that the existence of a target zone could reduce the probability that markets would test the boundaries of the exchange rate range.[52]

If a target zone for exchange rates could be established without significant cost, it would be desirable to do so. In practice, however, a number of considerations make it likely that proposals to limit exchange rates within well-defined ranges would be ineffective in achieving the stated objective or would entail costs that would outweigh any potential benefits.

In particular, there are reasons to doubt whether an effective target zone could be imposed without incurring a significant loss in domestic monetary independence. The argument that a target zone could be self-stabilizing follows from the initial theoretical model of a target zone.[53] A fully credible target zone would change the relationship between the exchange rate and the economic fundamentals in such a manner that the impact of unfavorable movements in the fundamentals on the exchange rate would weaken as the rate moves toward the edge of the band; hence, market participants would help to maintain the exchange rate within the band. The implication is that the loss of monetary independence caused by the imposition of a target zone could be substantially smaller than what might be expected from past experience. Subsequent work has made clear, however, that this result depends upon the assumption that the target zone is fully credible. If it is not, the relationship between the target zone and the fundamentals becomes more complex. The empirical work on target zones surveyed in Svensson (1992) suggests that, while the relationship between the exchange rate and the fundamentals appears to be somewhat different from what would be predicted under a free float, a target zone "appears very similar to a 'managed float' with a target central parity but without an explicit band." (Svensson (1992), p. 140).

The operation of a target zone would therefore involve some loss of domestic monetary independence, and there is little evidence that the major industrial countries would be prepared to compromise their domestic objectives in this manner. Even if they were willing to do so, many analysts doubt whether a target zone would be beneficial. For example, the belief that a target zone provides a useful anchor for exchange rate expectations can be questioned. As most target zone proposals involve relatively wide bands and frequent reassessments of these ranges, it is not clear how this system would provide such an anchor. Similarly, the argument that a target zone would provide more symmetry in adjustment is open to doubt. The evidence does not indicate that international adjustment under the Bretton Woods exchange rate regime was faster or more symmetric.[54] Given this experience of regimes with fixed exchange rates, it is not clear that the operation of a target zone would generate the hoped-for benefits.

More fundamentally, many would argue that establishment of target zones for the three key currencies could actually harm the world economy. By focusing on exchange rates rather than on underlying macroeconomic policies, such a system runs the risk of directing attention to symptoms rather than diseases and could actually lessen the pressures for corrective action. In addition, while movements in the exchange rate are often a useful signal to policymakers, the macroeconomic discipline provided by a policy of stabilizing the exchange rate need not always be beneficial.

A significant amount of work has been done on the impact of different exchange rate regimes.[55]

---

[52]This is one of the key implications of the literature on target zones started by Krugman (1991). Svensson (1992) provides a review of the literature.

[53]Krugman (1991).

[54]Indeed, the collapse of the system is often attributed to the lack of these properties. See the discussion in Eichengreen (1993).

[55]For example, Canzoneri (1982) and Flood and Marion (1982).

Much of the recent empirical work has used international macroeconomic models to assess the benefits of different international regimes, including target zones.[56] The results from comparing a target zone to a regime based on domestic indicators, such as the money supply, have been mixed; they appear to depend upon the nature of the underlying disturbances and the way in which the different regimes are specified. While it is always possible to criticize such work, as it is very difficult to analyze the impact of a fundamental change in a monetary regime, the evidence that a successful target zone would improve macroeconomic stability does not appear to be strong.

Also, a number of practical considerations with regard to target zone agreements would have to be resolved. It would be necessary to reach agreement about the appropriate range of fluctuations in the chosen exchange rate (bilateral or effective) and, most important, the responsibilities of participants for keeping the exchange rate within that range. The size of the range would depend on whether the range was aimed primarily at limiting exchange rate misalignments, or whether it should also aim to reduce volatility. The former objective would imply relatively wide bands, with exchange rates allowed to vary significantly over the short term. The latter combination of objectives would imply a much narrower band, such as under the original ERM in Europe, but, as the example of the ERM shows, such a band would be less flexible in the face of perceived policy dilemmas.

In either case, it would also be necessary to agree on the underlying parities and on how these parities might be moved in the light of changes in economic fundamentals. Agreement on underlying parities could well prove to be difficult. Indicators of appropriate exchange rates, such as alternative measures of international cost competitiveness, often provide imprecise and somewhat conflicting answers.[57] Moreover, different country authorities may not always share a common view or interest in defining appropriate ranges for exchange rates. In the first half of 1994, for example, the U.S. and Japanese authorities were not in complete accord regarding the range of the bilateral exchange rate between the yen and the dollar that would both contribute to a gradual reduction of payments imbalances and avoid undermining the recovery of the Japanese economy.

Some agreement on the relationship between the agreed target ranges and the economic fundamentals would also be desirable, so that it would be understood that changes in the fundamentals would prompt discussion of the need for changes in the ranges. Otherwise, these ranges would be in danger of becoming too rigid. While clearly not inevitable, arrangements to limit exchange rate variability have a tendency to become less flexible over time. The problems of the ERM in 1992–93, for example, are generally believed to have stemmed, at least in part, from a reluctance to change parities following the upward pressure on the deutsche mark as a result of the macroeconomic consequences of German unification. Similarly, the collapse of the Bretton Woods system was marked by problems in agreeing on changes in parities.

Policies to Maintain Target Zones

Exchange Market Intervention

The essential ingredient required to make an exchange rate range credible and effective is a clear agreement on both the policies required to keep the exchange rate within this range and the responsibilities of the participating governments in implementing these policies. One approach to maintaining such a range is sterilized exchange market intervention. However, the consensus view, as embodied in the Jurgensen Report (Jurgensen (1983)), is that the influence of sterilized official intervention is generally short term and cannot be relied upon to have either a substantial or a durable influence on exchange rates. Subsequent to the Jurgensen Report, some studies have suggested that coordinated intervention might be more useful than was previously appreciated, particularly as a signaling device for the implementation of other policies.[58] However, the experience with quite massive interventions during the European exchange rate crises of 1992–93, as well as with other recent interventions, appear to confirm the thrust of the Jurgensen Report, namely, that there are relatively narrow limits to what intervention alone may be expected to achieve on a sustained basis. This does not imply, of course, that intervention is irrelevant for target zones; indeed, such zones would be superficial if the authorities were not prepared to intervene when exchange rates threatened to breach their limits. Also, if there were a commitment to use other, more basic policies to defend the zone, intervention could carry more weight in the market. Nevertheless, a wide range of experience clearly demonstrates that exchange market intervention by itself is not adequate to significantly affect exchange rates over an extended period of time.

---

[56] Much of this work is contained in the books edited by Bryant and others (1989) and Bryant, Hooper, and Mann (1993). Most of this work focuses on the implications for the participants; unfortunately, there is very little work on the effects on countries outside the target zone.

[57] Such indicators are described in Clark and others (1994).

[58] See in particular Dominguez and Frankel (1993).

V LIMITING EXCHANGE RATE VARIABILITY: THE TARGET ZONE METHOD

Capital Controls

One reason for the limited effectiveness of official intervention is the expansion in private capital markets over time. As the magnitude of private foreign exchange market transactions has increased, the ability of governments to influence these markets through intervention has declined. This has led some observers, most notably James Tobin, to propose taxing international capital transactions or requiring the opening of interest-free deposits at the central bank by those undertaking capital transactions, with the aim of putting "sand in the wheels" of the capital markets.[59] Such a tax, it is argued, would increase the cost of speculation and, hence, the efficacy of official intervention. However, as with all capital controls, such a tax would also limit useful capital market transactions. There is no clear-cut way to separate inappropriate speculation and socially unproductive capital flows from those that are desirable. If restrictions based on taxes are not successful in distinguishing between productive and unproductive flows, many of the benefits of liberalization will be sacrificed, including increased returns to savers, lower costs of capital to firms, and better hedging instruments. Moreover, given the fungibility of capital and the ease with which taxed transactions can move offshore, it is not even clear that such a tax would be effective in limiting exchange rate volatility. While international capital markets may not always work perfectly, it is clear that they provide significant efficiency gains. The objective of reforms should therefore be to enhance their operations, not to limit them.

More generally, it may be noted that transactions costs, especially in stock markets, have declined precipitously over the course of this century as technology has improved. This decline in transactions costs has been associated with a massive increase in trading volumes in virtually all forms of marketable assets. Studies of the behavior of asset price volatility, however, do not reveal any upward trend, although the degree of volatility has varied to some extent from one decade to the next. This evidence does not suggest that a tax on transactions would be an effective method of reducing asset price volatility; indeed, it is difficult to see how taxes on transactions could lower asset price volatility, unless the taxes were set sufficiently high as to virtually eliminate these markets.

Fiscal Policy

Consideration could be given to deploying fiscal policy as an instrument to keep exchange rates within desired ranges. Again, however, there would seem to be formidable difficulties. First, the magnitude—and possibly even the sign—of the effect of fiscal policy on the exchange rate is uncertain and may change with special circumstances. The usual presumption is that expansionary fiscal actions result in an appreciation of the domestic currency; however, this may not be the case if the fiscal expansion undermined the credibility of government policies, in particular with regard to inflation. Furthermore, situations might arise in which the confidence-building effect of fiscal consolidation might induce exchange rate appreciation when such appreciation was not desirable.

Second, and more generally, it may be asked whether a system of target zones for the major currencies would usually operate in the right direction in terms of disciplining errant fiscal policies. When a country with a large fiscal deficit sees its currency depreciate excessively, the traditional advice given is to cut the deficit, both for its own sake and to alleviate pressures in the exchange market. Such traditional advice is based on the presumption that the confidence effect of cutting the deficit will outweigh the direct effect of budgetary consolidation on the real exchange rate. Many countries in this situation—including some industrial countries—have properly interpreted exchange rate depreciation as sending a message about the need for fiscal consolidation. It is far from clear, however, that exchange rate movements will consistently send the right messages about desirable adjustments of fiscal policies, especially to the three largest industrial countries. The United States in the mid-1980s is one example of this problem; it is unclear whether a much-needed move toward fiscal consolidation at that time would have made the overvalued dollar weaker or stronger. Another example is Japan in 1993–94, when an expansionary fiscal policy was being used to combat recession, and when a sharp appreciation of the yen helped to undermine an incipient economic recovery. What message was the appreciation of the yen sending to Japanese fiscal policy in that situation? Should Japanese fiscal policy have been tightened, in line with the normal presumption about the effects of fiscal policy on the exchange rate? Would a tightening of Japanese fiscal policy have made any sense in view of the cyclical situation in Japan and in other industrial countries, and in view of Japan's substantial current account surplus?

Moreover, even if the impact of fiscal policy on the exchange rate were known with reasonable certainty, the inflexibility of fiscal policy would remain as an important limitation on its use for exchange rate stabilization. Large exchange rate movements often occur relatively quickly with little or no advance warning, while fiscal policy is generally adjusted on a less frequent basis and often requires legislative

---

[59]See Tobin (1978).

approval. Fiscal policy also has its own important objectives, which should significantly limit its availability for exchange rate stabilization. For example, many industrial countries are currently engaged in medium-term programs to reduce their fiscal deficits and their ratios of government debt to GDP. The implementation of appropriate fiscal policies may well contribute indirectly to greater stability in exchange rates by making the domestic economic environment more predictable and by providing more flexibility for monetary authorities. However, the direct use of fiscal policy as a primary tool for exchange rate stabilization appears to be neither likely nor appropriate.

The principal benefit of fiscal consolidation in industrial countries is to strike a better balance between world saving and investment. By boosting the level of world saving, such consolidation would lead to lower real interest rates, greater productive investment, and higher growth in real output. Furthermore, these benefits would be worldwide, reaching well beyond the countries actually implementing such policies. As transmitted through the international monetary system, the implications of a country's economic policies and performance for other countries are therefore by no means limited to exchange rates alone.

The Role of Monetary Policy

As an instrument for maintaining exchange rate stability under the proposed target zones, monetary policy is the obvious candidate. It has the short-term flexibility required to respond to day-to-day events, and it is generally acknowledged to be among the more important determinants of exchange rate behavior. Also, countries that have successfully pegged their exchange rates over long periods of time have generally done so by targeting their monetary policies to this objective. This approach has usually entailed keeping domestic interest rates close to those in the foreign country to which the exchange rate is pegged, although, on occasion, it has required the adjustment of domestic interest rates to maintain the exchange rate peg.

Clearly, there are circumstances in which the conduct of monetary policy can be improved by constraining it through a commitment to stabilize a nominal exchange rate. This is essentially the "monetary discipline" argument in favor of pegged exchange rates or of target zones. When a country has difficulty in committing its monetary policy convincingly to the objective of maintaining reasonable price stability in the medium term, pegging the exchange rate of its currency to a partner country with an established reputation for price stability can be a very useful policy discipline. This was the experience of several European countries that pegged their exchange rates to the deutsche mark in successful efforts to bring down domestic inflation. It has also been the experience of a number of developing countries that have used exchange rate anchors in stabilization programs to reduce inflation dramatically.[60]

However, the situation in the largest industrial countries is not comparable to that of smaller countries, whose significant inflation problems could be addressed through a nominal exchange rate peg. After the upsurge of inflation in the 1970s and the costly but necessary efforts at disinflation in the 1980s, the three largest industrial countries have generally maintained relatively low inflation rates. When upsurges of inflation threatened in the late 1980s and early 1990s, all of these countries tightened monetary policies to contain the inflationary threat; moreover, inflation in these countries is falling toward the lowest rates recorded in the past three decades. In all three countries, there appears to be a firm commitment to use monetary policies to achieve reasonable price stability in the medium term. Accordingly, the idea that exchange rate discipline would be valuable in guarding against inflationary monetary policies does not appear to be particularly relevant to the situation of the largest industrial countries.

Moreover, orienting monetary policy toward exchange rate stabilization has distinct disadvantages. Because it is also the most flexible and timely instrument available for achieving domestic policy objectives, any use of monetary policy to limit exchange rate variability would inevitably reduce its flexibility to address domestic concerns. This dilemma was brought out most clearly in the European exchange rate turbulence of 1992–93. The anchor country in the system, Germany, was pursuing a policy of relatively high interest rates to resist inflationary pressures caused by the fiscal expansion following German unification. Such a policy was clearly less appropriate for countries that were experiencing economic downturns, most notably the United Kingdom and the Nordic countries. The perceived conflict between the relatively high interest rates required to maintain the exchange rate peg and the lower interest rates needed to revive domestic activity was clearly an important element in the market pressures in 1992 and 1993.

If such tensions were true in Europe, with its high level of intra-EU trade and integration, it is likely to be even more of a problem across the three largest industrial countries. To illustrate the difficulties involved, consider the situation in the summer of 1992, just before the beginning of the exchange rate

---

[60]For an analysis of their experience, see Bruno (1993), Calvo and Végh (1994), and Végh (1992).

V LIMITING EXCHANGE RATE VARIABILITY: THE TARGET ZONE METHOD

turmoil in Europe, when the U.S. dollar fell to a new low against the deutsche mark. This movement, which some regarded as excessive and undesirable, was at least in part a result of the different cyclical positions of the two economies. Monetary policy in Germany was relatively tight, while the weakness of the economic recovery and the low level of inflation in the United States led the Federal Reserve to continue to ease monetary conditions through the first half of 1992. Ultimately, the federal funds rate was pushed down to 3 percent in August 1992. To keep the dollar from depreciating as much as it did against the deutsche mark would have required a change in the actual or perceived monetary policy objectives either in Germany, which would have had to relax its anti-inflationary stance, or in the United States, which would have had to focus less on the domestic recovery. In both cases, such a change in economic policy would appear to have been neither popular nor economically desirable.

The history of the past 20 years supplies other important examples where the targeting of monetary policy on the exchange rate could have interfered with appropriate domestic objectives of monetary policy. In addition, to the extent that the commitment of monetary policy to exchange rate objectives might have undermined the achievement of growth and price stability objectives in the largest industrial countries, the harmful effects would probably not have been limited to these countries alone.

VI Conclusions and Implications for the IMF

The current international monetary system is one in which countries have exercised the considerable freedom of choice available to them with respect to exchange rate arrangements, against the background of a large and increasingly integrated global capital market. The three largest industrial countries have opted for a managed floating exchange rate regime. Apparently, they have come to the view that whatever the potential advantages of official actions to reduce exchange rate fluctuations, the costs associated with reduced monetary policy independence are sufficiently heavy to stop them from establishing a regime whereby they would be committed to keeping exchange rates within relatively narrow, announced ranges. When exchange rate misalignments are judged to be large, these countries have temporarily elevated exchange rate objectives over the domestic requirements of monetary policy—but such circumstances have been the exception rather than the rule.

It needs to be recognized, of course, that the behavior of each of the currencies of the three largest countries is not a matter of indifference for the other industrial countries, the developing countries, or the economies in transition. Fluctuations in the exchange rates of the former, as with other key macroeconomic variables, such as output and interest rates, have spillover effects on the rest of the IMF membership. It is therefore particularly important that these external repercussions be given explicit attention in the IMF surveillance described below. Helping to ensure that the economic fundamentals are sound in the three largest industrial countries will make a major contribution to improved economic performance in the world economy and thereby to exchange rate stability.

Quite legitimately, however, some other countries take a different view with regard to their own exchange rate arrangements. The implications of high exchange rate variability for their ongoing integration efforts, as well as the expected symmetry of shocks and the benefits of using the exchange rate as a nominal anchor, are seen as sufficient to motivate more ambitious forms of exchange rate management. Members of the ERM and many developing countries are good cases in point, although the problems experienced by the ERM in 1992–93 illustrate the difficult policy requirements needed to maintain such arrangements. There appears to be no compelling reason why such differences in views across countries about optimal exchange arrangements should not continue to coexist.

Given these considerations, it appears likely that changes in the international monetary system will be evolutionary rather than revolutionary. However, this need not mean that there is little scope for improvement in the functioning of the system. After the bitter experience with inflation in the 1970s and the costs of disinflation in the 1980s, the major industrial countries seem to have learned (or relearned) the importance of assuring that monetary policy is appropriately directed toward maintaining reasonable price stability in the medium term. This is reflected in the recent convergence of inflation rates in virtually all of the industrial countries to the lowest levels in three decades—and in these countries' apparent determination to preserve this key accomplishment. Recent progress has also been made in reducing fiscal imbalances and in beginning to put the ratios of public debt to GDP on a clearly downward course, although progress in these areas has been less pervasive than in the widespread reduction in inflation.

On the structural impediments to noninflationary growth, a good deal has been accomplished in liberalizing financial markets—as noted above—and in reforming the international trading system, but much remains to be done in the area of labor markets. Nevertheless, it is encouraging that improving the functioning of labor markets is increasingly being recognized as the key to reducing high levels of structural unemployment. Thus, on balance, the policy fundamentals for the convergence of the industrial countries to sustainable paths of noninflationary growth appear to be improving. This convergence in turn may be expected to remove one of the important sources of the volatility and misalignment of key exchange rates.

Moreover, following the large overvaluation of the dollar in the mid-1980s and the clear recognition of

VI CONCLUSIONS AND IMPLICATIONS FOR THE IMF

the costs associated with it, the major industrial countries have shown their resolve to resist a repetition of such problems—whether caused by deficient policies or by market excesses. The success of efforts at policy coordination is hard to judge and is open to some question with regard to the reduction of shorter-term exchange rate volatility; however, there is broad agreement that wide divergences of exchange rates from values plausibly implied by economic fundamentals cannot be treated with complete policy indifference. By itself, sterilized official intervention in foreign exchange markets is understood to be a tool of only limited effectiveness. It can sometimes be used successfully in a supporting role to send signals to the market, particularly to correct misconceptions about the views and intentions of policy authorities. When inappropriate policies appear to be contributing to exchange rate misalignments, peer pressure exerted through international coordination may help to move national policies in the right direction. When market forces seem to be driving exchange rates far from economic fundamentals, a united show of force by the authorities—encompassing both intervention and some policy adjustments—may be useful in counteracting bandwagon effects and other market excesses.

For the authorities of the three largest industrial countries, the key monetary and fiscal policy tools are generally perceived to have domestic objectives that are too important to allow the diversion of these policies primarily to efforts to defend relatively narrow exchange rate ranges. For these countries, sacrificing domestic economic stability to pursue a narrow concept of exchange rate stability would probably be harmful from a worldwide, as well as from a domestic, economic perspective. Accordingly, fundamental reform of the present international monetary system by transforming it into a system of target zones for the exchange rates of the major currencies is neither feasible nor desirable.

Realistically, reform of the international monetary system would better serve the fundamental purposes of the system by seeking continued improvement in the basic economic policies that create an environment for high, sustainable rates of noninflationary growth. The policy authorities of the largest industrial countries need first and foremost to keep their own houses in order. By avoiding disruptive cycles of inflation and disinflation, by achieving and maintaining sustainable fiscal positions, and by pursuing appropriate structural reforms, the governments of the largest countries will contribute not only to the growth and stability of their own economies but also to that of the entire world. International coordination that deals broadly with macroeconomic policy issues (rather than focusing narrowly on exchange rates) can contribute to this effort to secure and sustain better policies. The special contribution of such coordination should be to emphasize the international implications and interactions of domestic policies and to direct attention and peer pressure against policies that are inappropriate from both a domestic and international perspective.

Better policies should contribute in turn to greater stability in financial markets, including foreign exchange markets. Conversely, instabilities in financial markets often convey information that is relevant for economic policies. While foreign exchange markets are not unique in this regard, movements in exchange rates among the major currencies can be an important signal of either policy inadequacies or apparent departures of market forces from underlying economic fundamentals. In these circumstances, exchange rates should properly be an important focus of international policy coordination, even if the objective of such coordination is not generally to confine the exchange rates of the major independent currencies to narrowly prescribed ranges. By promoting better policies in the largest industrial countries and better international coordination of these policies—including an appropriate focus on exchange rates—it should be possible to achieve a more stable international monetary system that more effectively facilitates the growth of world trade, production, and welfare.

Under Article IV, Section 3(*a*) of its Articles of Agreement, the IMF is identified as the central institution with responsibility to "...oversee the international monetary system in order to ensure its effective operation...." Accordingly, the IMF has a significant role to play in efforts to improve the functioning of that system. In particular, through its exercise of surveillance, the IMF seeks to collaborate with its members in their efforts to pursue economic and financial policies that, as stated in Article IV, Section 1, support "...orderly economic growth with reasonable price stability..." and that "...promote stability by fostering orderly underlying economic and financial conditions and a monetary system that does not tend to produce erratic disruptions." Thus, the essential objective of IMF surveillance is the improvement of the international monetary system through better economic policies (especially in the largest countries) and better international coordination of these policies. Improved analysis of economic policies and performance, more timely diagnosis of problems as they begin to emerge, and more persuasive advice on how to avoid or correct such problems can contribute to the effectiveness of surveillance.

As indicated in Article IV, Section 3(*b*) of the Articles, the IMF has a special responsibility to

Conclusions and Implications for the IMF

exercise "firm surveillance" over the exchange rate policies of its members within its overall mandate for surveillance. From the perspective of improving the functioning of the international monetary system, probably the most important task of the IMF in this special area of responsibility is identifying potentially serious exchange rate misalignments at a relatively early stage, together with recommending corrective measures that might help to avoid more costly resolutions of such misalignments through market forces. In the case of pegged exchange rate regimes, identifying misalignments generally means recognizing situations in which political reluctance to change established nominal exchange rates is creating serious disequilibria in real exchange rates that are not likely to be corrected without a nominal exchange rate adjustment. This, of course, is an old problem; however, recent experience indicates that it is still a very relevant one. The solution lies in accurately diagnosing the problem and communicating (confidentially) the perhaps unpopular message that the problem exists and requires correction.

In the case of floating rate regimes, misalignments can reflect two sometimes reinforcing difficulties: inappropriate or conflicting policies, and market exuberances that push exchange rates out of line with underlying fundamentals. Surveillance that identifies and advises correction of inappropriate policies is the IMF's proper contribution to resolving the first of these difficulties. While IMF surveillance has admittedly not always been completely effective, this should not discourage its vigorous use or renewed efforts to strengthen it, including by emphasizing the role of the Interim Committee in such strengthened surveillance. The substantial uncertainty about equilibrium levels or ranges for exchange rates makes diagnosis difficult, and remedies are not always easily at hand. Nevertheless, experience suggests that circumstances do arise in which substantial exchange rate misalignments may plausibly be identified. Again, the lack of fully effective means to prevent market-driven misalignments should not be a barrier to reasonable attempts to counteract such misalignments when they are judged to be occurring. "Perfection" in the functioning of the international monetary system is not an achievable, or even a well-defined goal, and misguided pursuit of such perfection at the expense of other critically important policy objectives would be a mistake. Enhancing the effectiveness of IMF surveillance through improved analysis and more effective cooperation with and among the membership is the key contribution that the IMF can make to the evolutionary improvement in the international monetary system.

A narrow focus on the surveillance of exchange rates would be unwise. Policies that contribute to cycles of inflation and disinflation and to unnecessarily wide swings in output and employment, especially in the largest countries, will generally be a source of disturbance to the rest of the world regardless of the nature of the exchange rate regime. Surveillance that concentrates on exchange rates as the only important indicator of maladjusted policies and as the exclusive basis for policy coordination will often miss the point and could sometimes push policies in the wrong direction. Surveillance needs to have a broad focus, covering all key economic policies and all important indicators of actual or potential economic problems—including, but not limited to, exchange rates.

With the increasing international mobility of capital and the integration of capital markets, proper surveillance must also pay serious attention to developments in world financial markets. A number of recent episodes have demonstrated the importance of international financial markets as both a transmitter of economic disturbances and an evaluator of policies. Examples include the onset of the debt crisis in the early 1980s, the stock market crash of October 1987, and the sharp upward move in long-term interest rates in early 1994. Moreover, the efficient functioning of international financial markets is itself an essential requirement for a properly functioning international monetary system. Improved accounting and disclosure standards that would provide investors and creditors with better information on the creditworthiness of borrowers would assist the efficient functioning of these markets and, accordingly, is relevant to the IMF's general surveillance responsibilities. Even more important is the development and maintenance of adequate safeguards to contain and control potential systemic risks to the stability of international financial markets and, hence, to the stability of the international monetary system.

Finally, a key line of defense against an inappropriate transmission and magnification of economic disturbances is the availability of adequate external financing for countries that experience temporary balance of payments difficulties. The IMF continues to play an important role in this regard by making its general resources temporarily available, under adequate safeguards, in order, as noted in Article I of the Articles of Agreement, to provide its members " . . . with the opportunity to correct maladjustments in their balance of payments without resorting to measures destructive of national or international prosperity." For most IMF members, however, the initial and quantitatively most important source of external financing must be either the member's reserves or resources available through international borrowing. The level of reserves is generally not a critical concern for members that

VI CONCLUSIONS AND IMPLICATIONS FOR THE IMF

enjoy—and can reasonably expect to continue to enjoy—unimpeded access to world capital markets. However, for those IMF members that are likely to have to rely primarily on their own resources in times of difficulty, adequacy of reserves is an important issue. Because a significant number of members still have low levels of reserves and face high costs in acquiring and holding them, a reasonable case can be made to supplement other sources of reserves through an SDR allocation.

References

Adams, Charles, Paul R. Fenton, and Flemming Larsen, "Potential Output in Major Industrial Countries," in *Staff Studies for the World Economic Outlook*, World Economic and Financial Surveys (Washington: International Monetary Fund, August 1987).

Aghevli, Bijan B., Mohsin S. Khan, and Peter J. Montiel, *Exchange Rate Policy in Developing Countries: Some Analytical Issues*, IMF Occasional Paper No. 78 (Washington: International Monetary Fund, March 1991).

Aizenman, Joshua, "Exchange Rate Flexibility, Volatility, and Domestic and Foreign Direct Investment," *Staff Papers*, International Monetary Fund, Vol. 39 (December 1992), pp. 890–922.

Alesina, A., V. Grilli, and G.M. Milesi-Ferreti, "The Political Economy of Capital Controls," in *Capital Mobility: The Impact on Consumption, Investment, and Growth*, ed. by L. Leiderman and A. Razin (Cambridge, England: Cambridge University Press, 1994).

Barrell, Ray, and Simon Wren-Lewis, "Fundamental Equilibrium Exchange Rates for the G7," CEPR Discussion Paper No. 323 (London: Center for Economic Policy Research, June 1989).

Bayoumi, Tamim, *One Money or Many: On Analyzing the Prospects for Monetary Unification in Various Parts of the World*, Essays in International Finance, No. 76, Princeton University (Princeton, New Jersey: Princeton University Press, 1994).

———, and Barry Eichengreen, "Macroeconomic Adjustment Under Bretton Woods and the Post-Bretton Woods Float: An Impulse Response Analysis," *Economic Journal*, Vol. 104 (July 1994), pp. 813–27.

Bordo, Michael D., "The Bretton Woods International Monetary System: An Historical Overview," in *A Retrospective on the Bretton Woods System: Lessons for International Monetary Reform*, ed. by Michael D. Bordo and Barry Eichengreen (Chicago and London: University of Chicago Press, 1993).

———, and Barry Eichengreen, eds., *A Retrospective on the Bretton Woods System: Lessons for International Monetary Reform* (Chicago and London: University of Chicago Press, 1993).

Bruno, Michael, *Crisis, Stabilization and Economic Reform* (Oxford: Clarendon Press, 1993).

Bryant, Ralph C., and others, eds., *Macroeconomic Policies in an Interdependent World* (Washington: Brookings Institution, 1989).

Bryant, Ralph C., Peter Hooper, and Catherine L. Mann, eds., *Evaluating Policy Regimes: New Research in Empirical Macroeconomics* (Washington: Brookings Institution, 1993).

Calvo, Guillermo A., and Carlos Végh, "Inflation Stabilization and Nominal Anchors," *Contemporary Economic Policy*, Vol. 12 (April 1994), pp. 35–45.

Canzoneri, Matthew B. "Exchange Intervention Policy in a Multiple Country World," *Journal of International Economics*, Vol. 13 (November 1982), pp. 267–89.

Clark, Peter, and others, *Exchange Rates and Economic Fundamentals: A Framework for Analysis*, IMF Occasional Paper No. 116 (Washington: International Monetary Fund, December 1994).

Coats, Warren L., Reinhard W. Furstenberg, and Peter Isard, *The SDR System and the Issue of Resource Transfers*, Essays in International Finance, No. 180, Princeton University (Princeton, New Jersey: Princeton University Press, 1990).

Commission of the European Communities, "One Market, One Money: An Evaluation of the Potential Benefits and Costs of Forming an Economic and Monetary Union," *European Economy*, No. 44 (Brussels: Commission of the European Communities, October 1990).

Crockett, Andrew, and Morris Goldstein, *Strengthening the International Monetary System: Exchange Rates, Surveillance, and Objective Indicators*, IMF Occasional Paper No. 50 (Washington: International Monetary Fund, February 1987).

Dominguez, Kathryn M., and Jeffrey A. Frankel, *Does Foreign Exchange Rate Intervention Work?* (Washington: Institute for International Economics, September 1993).

Eichengreen, Barry, "Real Exchange Rate Behavior Under Alternative Exchange Rate Regimes: Interwar Evidence," *European Economic Review*, Vol. 32 (March 1988), pp. 363–71.

———, "Epilogue: Three Perspectives on the Bretton Woods System," in *A Retrospective on the Bretton Woods System: Lessons for International Monetary Reform*, ed. by Michael D. Bordo and Barry Eichengreen (Chicago and London: University of Chicago Press, 1993).

El-Erian, Mohammed, "The Regulation and Supervision of Cross-Border Banking," (unpublished; Washington: International Monetary Fund, 1992).

Feldstein, Martin, "Thinking about International Coordination," *Journal of Economic Perspectives*, Vol. 2 (Spring 1988), pp. 3–13.

Fishlow, Albert, "Lessons from the Past: Capital Markets During the 19th Century and Interwar Period,"

REFERENCES

Industrial Organization, Vol. 39 (Summer 1985), pp. 383–439.

Flood, Robert P. and Nancy Marion, "Transmission of Disturbances under Alternative Exchange-Rate Regimes with Optimal Indexation," *Quarterly Journal of Economics*, No. 97 (February 1982), pp. 43–68.

Frankel, Jeffrey A., and Shang-Jin Wei, "Trade Blocs and Currency Blocs," NBER Working Paper No. 4335 (Cambridge, Massachusetts: National Bureau of Economic Research, April 1993).

Frenkel, Jacob A., and Morris Goldstein, "Guide to Target Zones," *Staff Papers*, International Monetary Fund, Vol. 33 (December 1986), pp. 633–73.

———, "Macroeconomic Policy Implications of Currency Zones," in *Policy Implications of Trade and Currency Zones* (Kansas City: Federal Reserve Bank of Kansas City, 1991).

———, and Paul Masson, *Characteristics of a Successful Exchange Rate System*, IMF Occasional Paper No. 82 (Washington: International Monetary Fund, July 1991).

Funabashi, Yoichi, *Managing the Dollar: From the Plaza to the Louvre* (Washington: Institute for International Economics, 1988).

Gagnon, Joseph E., "Exchange Rate Variability and the Level of International Trade," *Journal of International Economics*, Vol. 34 (May 1993), pp. 269–87.

Garber, Peter, "The Collapse of the Bretton Woods Fixed Exchange Rate System," in *A Retrospective on the Bretton Woods System*, ed. by Michael D. Bordo and Barry Eichengreen (Chicago and London: University of Chicago Press, 1993).

Goldberg, Linda, "Exchange Rates and Investment in United States Industry," *Review of Economics and Statistics*, Vol. 75 (November 1993), pp. 575–88.

Goldstein, Morris, and others, *Policy Issues in the Evolving International Monetary System*, IMF Occasional Paper No. 96 (Washington: International Monetary Fund, June 1992).

Goldstein, Morris, David Folkerts-Landau, and others, (1993a), *International Capital Markets: Part I. Exchange Rate Management and International Capital Flows*, World Economic and Financial Surveys (Washington: International Monetary Fund, April 1993).

——— (1993b), *International Capital Markets: Part II. Systemic Issues in International Finance*, World Economic and Financial Surveys (Washington: International Monetary Fund, August 1993).

Goldstein, Morris, and Michael Mussa, "The Integration of World Capital Markets," IMF Working Paper, WP/93/95 (Washington: International Monetary Fund, December 1993).

Goldstein, Morris, David Folkerts-Landau, and others, *International Capital Markets: Developments, Prospects, and Policy Issues*, World Economic and Financial Surveys (Washington: International Monetary Fund, September 1994).

Group of Ten Deputies, *International Capital Movements and Foreign Exchange Markets: Report to the Ministers and Governors by the Group of Ten Deputies* (Rome: Bank of Italy, April 1993).

International Monetary Fund (1984a), *Exchange Rate Volatility and the Level of International Trade*, IMF Occasional Paper No. 28 (Washington: International Monetary Fund, July 1984).

——— (1984b), *Issues in the Assessment of the Exchange Rates of Industrial Countries*, IMF Occasional Paper No. 29 (Washington: International Monetary Fund, July 1984).

——— (1984c), *The Exchange Rate System: Lessons of the Past and Options for the Future*, IMF Occasional Paper No. 30 (Washington: International Monetary Fund, July 1984).

———, *The Role of the SDR in the International Monetary System*, IMF Occasional Paper No. 51 (Washington: International Monetary Fund, March 1987).

———, *Exchange Arrangements and Exchange Restrictions: Annual Report 1993* (Washington: International Monetary Fund, 1993).

———, *International Financial Statistics*, various issues.

Jurgensen, P., "Report of the Working Group on Exchange Market Intervention," (Washington: U.S. Treasury Department, March 1983).

Krugman, Paul, "Louvre's Lesson: Let the Dollar Fall," *The International Economy*, (January/February 1988), pp. 76–82.

———, "The Case for Stabilizing Exchange Rates," *Oxford Review of Economic Policy*, Vol. 5 (Autumn 1989), pp. 61–72.

———, "Target Zones and Exchange Rate Dynamics," *Quarterly Journal of Economics*, Vol. 106 (August 1991), pp. 669–82.

Maddison, Angus, *Dynamic Forces in Capitalist Development: A Long-Run Cooperative View* (Oxford and New York: Oxford University Press, 1991).

Mundell, Robert A., "A Theory of Optimum Currency Areas," *American Economic Review*, Vol. 51 (September 1961), pp. 657–65.

Mussa, Michael L., *Exchange Rates in Theory and in Reality*, Essays in International Finance, No. 179, Princeton University (Princeton, New Jersey: Princeton University Press, 1990).

Rhomberg, Rudolf R., "Failings of the SDR: Lessons from Three Decades," in *International Financial Policy: Essays in Honor of Jacques J. Polak*, ed. by Jacob Frenkel and Morris Goldstein (Washington: International Monetary Fund and De Nederlandsche Bank, 1991).

Schadler, Susan, Maria Carkovic, Alan Bennett, and Robert Khan, *Recent Experiences with Surges in Capital Inflows*, IMF Occasional Paper No. 108 (Washington: International Monetary Fund, December 1993).

Shleifer, Andrei, and Lawrence H. Summers, "The Noise Trader Approach to Finance," *The Journal of Economic Perspectives*, Vol. 4, No. 2 (Spring 1990), pp. 19–33.

Solomon, Robert, *The International Monetary System, 1945–1981* (New York: Harper & Row, 1982).

Svensson, Lars E.O., "An Interpretation of Recent Research on Exchange Rate Target Zones," *The Journal of Economic Perspectives*, Vol. 6 (Fall 1992), pp. 119–44.

Tavlas, George, "The 'New' Theory of Optimum Currency Areas," *The World Economy*, Vol. 16 (November 1993), pp. 663–85.

Tobin, James, "A Proposal for International Monetary Reform," Cowles Foundation Discussion Paper No. 506 (New Haven: Cowles Foundation for Research in Economics at Yale University, October 1978).

Ungerer, Horst, and others, *The European Monetary System: Recent Developments*, IMF Occasional Paper No. 48 (Washington: International Monetary Fund, December 1986).

———, *The European Monetary System: Developments and Prospectives*, IMF Occasional Paper No. 74 (Washington: International Monetary Fund, December 1990).

Végh, Carlos, "Stopping High Inflation," *Staff Papers*, International Monetary Fund, Vol. 39 (September 1992), pp. 626–95.

Williamson, John, *The Exchange Rate System*, Policy Analyses in International Economics, No. 5 (Washington: Institute for International Economics, 2nd ed., 1985).

———, and Marcus Miller, *Targets and Indicators: A Blueprint for International Coordination of Economic Policy* (Washington, Institute for International Economics, 1987).

———, and C. Randall Henning, "Managing the Monetary System," paper presented at a conference on "Managing the World Economy," Washington, May 1994.

OCCASIONAL PAPERS

Recent Occasional Papers of the International Monetary Fund

116. Improving the International Monetary System: Constraints and Possibilities, by Michael Mussa, Morris Goldstein, Peter B. Clark, Donald J. Mathieson, and Tamim Bayoumi. 1994.
115. Exchange Rates and Economic Fundamentals: A Framework for Analysis, by Peter B. Clark, Leonardo Bartolini, Tamim Bayoumi, and Steven Symansky. 1994.
114. Economic Reform in China: A New Phase, by Wanda Tseng, Hoe Ee Khor, Kalpana Kochhar, Dubravko Mihaljek, and David Burton. 1994.
113. Poland: The Path to a Market Economy, by Liam P. Ebrill, Ajai Chopra, Charalambos Christofides, Paul Mylonas, Inci Otker, and Gerd Schwartz. 1994.
112. The Behavior of Non-Oil Commodity Prices, by Eduardo Borensztein, Mohsin S. Khan, Carmen M. Reinhart, and Peter Wickham. 1994.
111. The Russian Federation in Transition: External Developments, by Benedicte Vibe Christensen. 1994.
110. Limiting Central Bank Credit to the Government: Theory and Practice, by Carlo Cottarelli. 1993.
109. The Path to Convertibility and Growth: The Tunisian Experience, by Saleh M. Nsouli, Sena Eken, Paul Duran, Gerwin Bell, and Zühtü Yücelik. 1993.
108. Recent Experiences with Surges in Capital Inflows, by Susan Schadler, Maria Carkovic, Adam Bennett, and Robert Kahn. 1993.
107. China at the Threshold of a Market Economy, by Michael W. Bell, Hoe Ee Khor, and Kalpana Kochhar with Jun Ma, Simon N'guiamba, and Rajiv Lall. 1993.
106. Economic Adjustment in Low-Income Countries: Experience Under the Enhanced Structural Adjustment Facility, by Susan Schadler, Franek Rozwadowski, Siddharth Tiwari, and David O. Robinson. 1993.
105. The Structure and Operation of the World Gold Market, by Gary O'Callaghan. 1993.
104. Price Liberalization in Russia: Behavior of Prices, Household Incomes, and Consumption During the First Year, by Vincent Koen and Steven Phillips. 1993.
103. Liberalization of the Capital Account: Experiences and Issues, by Donald J. Mathieson and Liliana Rojas-Suárez. 1993.
102. Financial Sector Reforms and Exchange Arrangements in Eastern Europe. Part I: Financial Markets and Intermediation, by Guillermo A. Calvo and Manmohan S. Kumar. Part II: Exchange Arrangements of Previously Centrally Planned Economies, by Eduardo Borensztein and Paul R. Masson. 1993.
101. Spain: Converging with the European Community, by Michel Galy, Gonzalo Pastor, and Thierry Pujol. 1993.
100. The Gambia: Economic Adjustment in a Small Open Economy, by Michael T. Hadjimichael, Thomas Rumbaugh, and Eric Verreydt. 1992.
99. Mexico: The Strategy to Achieve Sustained Economic Growth, edited by Claudio Loser and Eliot Kalter. 1992.
98. Albania: From Isolation Toward Reform, by Mario I. Blejer, Mauro Mecagni, Ratna Sahay, Richard Hides, Barry Johnston, Piroska Nagy, and Roy Pepper. 1992.
97. Rules and Discretion in International Economic Policy, by Manuel Guitián. 1992.
96. Policy Issues in the Evolving International Monetary System, by Morris Goldstein, Peter Isard, Paul R. Masson, and Mark P. Taylor. 1992.
95. The Fiscal Dimensions of Adjustment in Low-Income Countries, by Karim Nashashibi, Sanjeev Gupta, Claire Liuksila, Henri Lorie, and Walter Mahler. 1992.
94. Tax Harmonization in the European Community: Policy Issues and Analysis, edited by George Kopits. 1992.
93. Regional Trade Arrangements, by Augusto de la Torre and Margaret R. Kelly. 1992.

Occasional Papers

92. Stabilization and Structural Reform in the Czech and Slovak Federal Republic: First Stage, by Bijan B. Aghevli, Eduardo Borensztein, and Tessa van der Willigen. 1992.
91. Economic Policies for a New South Africa, edited by Desmond Lachman and Kenneth Bercuson with a staff team comprising Daudi Ballali, Robert Corker, Charalambos Christofides, and James Wein. 1992.
90. The Internationalization of Currencies: An Appraisal of the Japanese Yen, by George S. Tavlas and Yuzuru Ozeki. 1992.
89. The Romanian Economic Reform Program, by Dimitri G. Demekas and Mohsin S. Khan. 1991.
88. Value-Added Tax: Administrative and Policy Issues, edited by Alan A. Tait. 1991.
87. Financial Assistance from Arab Countries and Arab Regional Institutions, by Pierre van den Boogaerde. 1991.
86. Ghana: Adjustment and Growth, 1983–91, by Ishan Kapur, Michael T. Hadjimichael, Paul Hilbers, Jerald Schiff, and Philippe Szymczak. 1991.
85. Thailand: Adjusting to Success—Current Policy Issues, by David Robinson, Yangho Byeon, and Ranjit Teja with Wanda Tseng. 1991.
84. Financial Liberalization, Money Demand, and Monetary Policy in Asian Countries, by Wanda Tseng and Robert Corker. 1991.
83. Economic Reform in Hungary Since 1968, by Anthony R. Boote and Janos Somogyi. 1991.
82. Characteristics of a Successful Exchange Rate System, by Jacob A. Frenkel, Morris Goldstein, and Paul R. Masson. 1991.
81. Currency Convertibility and the Transformation of Centrally Planned Economies, by Joshua E. Greene and Peter Isard. 1991.
80. Domestic Public Debt of Externally Indebted Countries, by Pablo E. Guidotti and Manmohan S. Kumar. 1991.
79. The Mongolian People's Republic: Toward a Market Economy, by Elizabeth Milne, John Leimone, Franek Rozwadowski, and Padej Sukachevin. 1991.
78. Exchange Rate Policy in Developing Countries: Some Analytical Issues, by Bijan B. Aghevli, Mohsin S. Khan, and Peter J. Montiel. 1991.
77. Determinants and Systemic Consequences of International Capital Flows, by Morris Goldstein, Donald J. Mathieson, David Folkerts-Landau, Timothy Lane, J. Saúl Lizondo, and Liliana Rojas-Suárez. 1991.
76. China: Economic Reform and Macroeconomic Management, by Mario Blejer, David Burton, Steven Dunaway, and Gyorgy Szapary. 1991.
75. German Unification: Economic Issues, edited by Leslie Lipschitz and Donogh McDonald. 1990.
74. The Impact of the European Community's Internal Market on the EFTA, by Richard K. Abrams, Peter K. Cornelius, Per L. Hedfors, and Gunnar Tersman. 1990.
73. The European Monetary System: Developments and Perspectives, by Horst Ungerer, Jouko J. Hauvonen, Augusto Lopez-Claros, and Thomas Mayer. 1990.
72. The Czech and Slovak Federal Republic: An Economy in Transition, by Jim Prust and an IMF Staff Team. 1990.
71. MULTIMOD Mark II: A Revised and Extended Model, by Paul Masson, Steven Symansky, and Guy Meredith. 1990.
70. The Conduct of Monetary Policy in the Major Industrial Countries: Instruments and Operating Procedures, by Dallas S. Batten, Michael P. Blackwell, In-Su Kim, Simon E. Nocera, and Yuzuru Ozeki. 1990.
69. International Comparisons of Government Expenditure Revisited: The Developing Countries, 1975–86, by Peter S. Heller and Jack Diamond. 1990.
68. Debt Reduction and Economic Activity, by Michael P. Dooley, David Folkerts-Landau, Richard D. Haas, Steven A. Symansky, and Ralph W. Tryon. 1990.

Note: For information on the title and availability of Occasional Papers not listed, please consult the IMF *Publications Catalog* or contact IMF Publication Services.

HG 3881 .I349 1994

IMPROVING THE INTERNATIONAL